PEARSON ALWAYS LEARNING

Adnan Salhi

Crossing Boundaries

Pearson Learning Solutions, 501 Boylston Street, Suite 900, Boston, MA 02116
A Pearson Education Company
www.pearsoned.com

Printed in the United States of America

3 4 5 6 7 8 9 10 VOZN 17 16 15

000200010271935962

TS

ISBN 10: 1-323-03441-2
ISBN 13: 978-1-323-03441-5

Table of Contents

Foreword

This is the second book of students' personal stories to be published by Professor Salhi based on his Developmental Reading and Writing classes at Henry Ford College. The first book, *Reading Our Lives: Writing Our True Stories*, was the result of Salhi's belief that students would be more motivated to write if they wrote about themselves. In addition, they would be more motivated to read if they could read each other's stories. The resulting stories in the first book were amazingly truthful, very personal, and positively hopeful.

An unexpected benefit from these stories was the realization that the problems and obstacles in the students' lives could be overcome with determination and genuine help. These stories also provided a much needed insight into the students' state of development and their particular needs.

Because the first collection of student stories was so insightful and interesting, Salhi decided to publish them in a book. The next groups of Developmental Reading and Writing students used *Reading Our Lives: Writing Our True Stories* as one of their texts, and it proved to be very popular and highly motivating. These were people and situations that they could relate to—they recognized the situations they were reading about. With the help of what he learned from students' responses to the first book, Salhi modified his course material to further improve writing abilities. The result was definitely improved writing quality and still very personal and truthful stories. This, then, is the second publication of students' personal stories, called *Crossing Boundaries*. These stories are both amazing, considering the challenges the students faced in their lives, and uplifting because of their determination to succeed in spite of those challenges.

Edward Rishavy

Introduction

This book was inspired by the success my students and I had with our first book *Reading Our Lives: Writing Our True Stories.* Right after reading the introduction and one of the stories in the first book, several of them came up to me after class and said, "I really like this book and I want my story to be in it." As we progressed in reading the stories, students displayed an unusual immersion in the reading, engagement in the discussion, and interest in reading more of the stories.

When I asked the students about these phenomena, their responses were thrilling and revealing to me. Some of their responses included:

"I can relate to these stories."
"I can see myself in this book."
"I know the places and I can imagine what happens in them every day."
"This book is interesting. It keeps me awake and I want to read on."
"When I read the first story, I felt like I wanted to read all the stories in this book."

Students' reactions to *Reading Our Lives: Writing Our True Stories,* and their desire and demand to be included in it, lead me to work on this book, *Crossing Boundaries.* In reality, I felt an obligation to work on this book and publish it. I owed it to my students to publish this book for many reasons.

First, my students taught me that educators and policy makers had it wrong. In the past, we focused on whether or not students came to us with the proper degree of motivation to learn instead of focusing on how classroom experiences affected our students. Second, my students reemphasized to me that regardless of their poverty level, their low attendance, and the negative peer influence on them, there was a more powerful force that brought these students to the class and kept them in it. That force was the human element, the genuine empathy and the true affection these students needed. Many of my students graduate from my classes and come back to see me, to ask me for further help and guidance, or to tell me how much the class/classes we had together influenced their lives. Third, my students keep reminding me that the teacher's main role is to make learning joyful, to give students the courage to take risks, think, and express their thinking without fear of being labeled or judged. Fourth, my students reemphasized to me that they signed up for college classes because they were serious about learning and becoming somebody. The diligence they displayed in reading and writing and the emotions they displayed in telling their narratives were enough evidence to prove the seriousness of these students. In their daily interactions with me, my students challenged me, as a teacher, to rise up to their expectations and lend them the helping hand they needed to become positive builders in their homes, neighborhoods, and the larger communities they lived in.

The difficulties facing our students are immeasurable. From reading their stories, it becomes easy to understand how resilient and how determined to succeed these students are. When educators truly understand that the difficulties our students face are not limited to poverty, language skills, single parent households, limited community support, school violence, drug abuse, physical abuse, and sexual abuse, it becomes unfathomable when policy makers and educators do not do whatever it takes to help these students achieve their dreams. It becomes unfathomable to accept any attempt by anyone to close doors, cancel programs, or limit these students' access to the much-needed high quality education they deserve.

Any sensible person who reads the students' narratives and stories in *Reading Our Lives: Writing Our True Stories* or in *Crossing Boundaries* will understand that without the educators' genuine empathy and true affection, these students will have no real options for achieving decent lives. The stakes in attending college for these students are extremely high. Even though teaching these students can be, or will be, highly charged and exceptionally draining, it is certainly worth all the effort invested in this worthy cause.

Crossing Boundaries is a reflection of the borders our "developmental" students have to face in the USA. No matter what form these borders take, they are real, costly, and dangerous. Without support, these borders become insurmountable. Our students will use any kind of help that is genuinely sincere, and they will use it to succeed because they are determined to succeed.

Before I invite the readers to enter the lives of these brave writers, I want to thank my students for their hard work and dedication. I want to thank them for making me a better teacher and a better human being. I also want to thank my friends and scholars Richard Rogers, Mark Whitters, and Grant Shafer from Eastern Michigan University. I want to thank them for their priceless suggestions and comments that made this book look better. I am also very grateful to my wonderful friends Bill Turbett and Edward Rishavy. The time they spent in reviewing this book and contributing to it are deeply appreciated. It goes beyond saying that I am also grateful to my friend Rosalie Rishavy from Henry Ford College for her help and valuable suggestions. I also want to thank my wife, Maha Salhi, for her comments on all of the first drafts of these stories. My students and I found her suggestions thoughtful and useful.

Adnan Salhi

The Lesson

Adnan Salhi

～～～

When anyone walked in front of her house, anyone would notice the beautiful design and the variety of flowers and plants in her garden. Anyone could see the deep pride Officer Golden had taken in her accomplishments when she talked to her visitors about the beauty of her garden and what she had to do to make it look the way it did. When she talked about her garden, her talk revealed the fine taste, education, and style Officer Golden had acquired. Everyone liked to talk to her. How could one not when she had been mentioned in several of the community activities for being an exemplary role model in almost every aspect of her community life? Not only did Officer Golden enjoy her popularity in her small community, but she also enjoyed the love and support of her devoted husband and her successful son. Everyone who knew her envied her because she seemed to have it all.

On her day off from work, Officer Golden thought of going to the shopping mall. She did not know what she wanted to buy. She did not know if she actually needed to buy anything. It was 10 a.m., and she thought there was plenty of time before going to pray. Something was worrying her, but she did not know what it was or why it was on her mind. It kept her on edge and jittery. She wondered if she should go to prayer or to the store first. Going to the store finally prevailed. Her husband had told her that he would leave the house early and meet her at prayer. Her son was in college taking summer classes, and

1

he lived on campus because it was not practical for him to commute every day. Officer Golden was home alone when she put on some of her best clothes. She always dressed well and she always looked well. She was educated, well respected, and a charmer, people said. She looked at herself in the mirror for the last time before she left her home.

As she walked to her car, she felt the adrenaline rushing through her veins, but she did not know why. A ghost of an idea passed through her mind telling her to join her husband at prayer, but something kept telling her to go on with what she intended to do, and it was more vociferous, alluring, and irresistible. She proceeded to her car, oblivious to everything except what she had her mind set on doing. After all, she was a police officer, and no one could stand in her way. One idea took control of her mind and her body. She could not think or move in any way that might jeopardize what she set out to do.

In the parking lot, cars were standing motionless in the sizzling heat of the summer sun. She was the only one there when she thought of her destination, Macy's. She knew it was not going to be crowded because it was opening time. She would just pick up something for herself and head back to meet her husband. She had almost 90 minutes, plenty of time. She looked around her when she took her car keys out of her pocket. She opened the door and slipped into her car hastily, turned the car on, and proceeded to leave the parking area, turning west to take I-75. The streets were not crowded in her quiet town at this time of the day. Pedestrians crossed the street slowly. From her seat behind the steering wheel, she whimpered, urging the pedestrians, "Come on, people! Come on! Please move faster. Faster." No one listened to her or even heard her, but she did not stop admonishing them to move

2

faster every time she had to stop and wait for people to cross the street. She did not want to be late for prayer, and she did not want her husband to ask her why she was late, because she did not want to lie to him.

She exited I-75 and took the shortest way she knew to get to Macy's. She was not paying any attention to anything except being where she wanted to be as quickly as possible. She turned into the mall's parking area, parked her car in the nearest parking space she could find, and walked to the store feeling pumped up. She was two minutes early. As she waited for the door to open, the ghost of the idea entered her mind again to tell her that she still had time to join her husband. She was in tug of war. Going into the store was a passion, a preoccupation, and, she had to admit, a sickness that she could not resist. When the employee opened the door and greeted the waiting customers with a smile, Officer Golden smiled back and walked to the buggy rack in a rush. There were only a few people in the store. She walked around, looking and pushing her buggy between aisles into different sections of the store. She checked price tags, sprayed different perfumes on herself, tried on some shoes, and did other things. Every time she did something, for some reason, she felt that someone was watching her, and that annoyed her. "Why is that person looking at me like that?" she thought. "I wonder if I should just leave and come back again later," she went on thinking. She moved on and stopped at the belts. She tried one belt on, checked it out in a mirror, and liked it. She kept it for later on and continued moving and looking around in the store. She picked a couple pairs of sweat pants and decided to try them on in the fitting rooms. There was an employee at the counter in front of the fitting room. The employee gave her a number and directed her where to go. She tried the sweat pants but decided that she did not like them. She left the fitting room, gave the number and the pants to the employee, and decided to leave the store.

When she stepped outside and was about ten feet outside the store, she heard a voice that was familiar to her.

"Mom?" the familiar male voice said. The voice was similar to her son's, but he could not possibly be here. He was at the college; she was sure. She looked behind her, and there he was. Her son was standing at the door and looking at her in or disbelief. "Why did he address me in this formal way?" she wondered. Only she and her son were there.

"Step back here, please," her son said. When she did, her son said, "That belt you are wearing is not yours. You did not pay for it."

"Is this a joke?" she asked. Suddenly her mouth dried up. She had difficulty breathing, and she started sweating.

She did not know what to say to her son when he said, "The days I don't have classes, I work here. I work on the security cameras, and I watched you put the belt on without paying for it. I still can't believe what I saw."

"You must be out of your mind. I can't believe what I'm hearing," she said with a dry mouth.

"I wish I were out of my mind. Look at my hands! I'm still shaking from the shock. You're my role model. You're the one who taught me about God, honesty, morality. You're the one who taught me to read from the Holy Book. I could not believe that you taught me all this and did what you did. I wouldn't believe it if I hadn't seen it with my own eyes." Her son was fighting back tears as he said, "Please come inside the store with me."

"You must have made a mistake. I'm your mother. Please go and look at the tape one more time."

4

"Believe me, I looked at it several times when you were in the fitting room."

"You must have made a mistake!"

"No I haven't. I followed you closely from the moment you entered. In the beginning, I thought it was going to be a joke, but it turned out to be different. Why did you do this? You didn't need this belt. You can afford twenty like it. You give me money to help with my tuition. Why did you do this? Why would someone with so much to lose do something like that?" His eyes started welling before he added, "Look, I don't want to call the police. If you cooperate with me and step inside, I'll keep it quiet."

"Let's talk about this here. There must be a mistake," she insisted.

"I can't. Please don't make it harder. If you come with me, I won't call the police. If my boss comes in, this will be out of my hands, and I don't know what he'll do," he said as he tried to avoid looking into her eyes. Both of them were in disbelief. Seeing how adamant he was, and to avoid getting customers' attention, she walked with him inside the store. He took her with him to the observation room in the back of the store. The room was filled with monitors that showed customers in every corner of the store. The customers were walking, handling merchandise, checking prices of some, taking others off the racks, and examining price tags. She saw all that and more while she was in the room. The customers were unaware of how closely they were watched and how closely the camera could zoom in on them.

"Now that we are here, show me your proof," she nervously demanded.

He did not respond to what she said. One minute later, a young female employee came in and sat on a chair without uttering a word.

"Who is this?" his mother demanded.

"This is my witness. She will not utter a word. She'll just sit there to make sure that you are treated fairly and according to the law," he explained. When Officer Golden saw the grin on the woman's face, her humiliation was nonpareil and indelible.

"Do you know what you're doing to me? Do you know that I will lose my job because of this? Please think about what you are doing," she begged her unbent son.

"You will not lose your job, because the paper I want you to sign will not go anywhere outside this company. You will receive a civil demand letter in the mail asking you to pay for the merchandise and to stay away from the store for at least six months."

"Don't you understand that you are ruining me and my career by what you are doing? Don't you understand that you are also ruining your own family?" she pleaded again in a hoarse voice while tears were filling her eyes. He gave her a tissue and remained silent. He was immersed in deep thinking. When his colleague was called to the store floor, he addressed his mother solemnly,

"I can't go back on having you sign these papers, but I promise you that tomorrow I will give them to you and you can do with them whatever you want. It will be as if nothing had happened. This will stay between us, and no one will ever know about it. Please sign the papers before my boss comes in. Once he comes in, I will not be able to control what will happen."

Sobbing, scared, and eager to get out of this humiliating situation, she said, "Give me the papers to sign. I hope you will review your tapes and see that you accused me falsely."

He filled out two forms and gave them to her to sign. When she did, he called on one of the employees and asked her to give him a price on the belt. It was $25.00. He attached

6

the receipt to the forms, made copies of all the papers, gave them to her, and said, "Tomorrow you will have the originals. You can go now." She walked out without looking back. She did not know what had compelled her to go to the store at that time. She stared in disbelief as she faced up to her painful humiliation. Her mind was swirling with the questions, "Why? Why did this happen to me? Was it for the thrill of it? It could not be. My job gives me too much of a thrill, and I don't need more. Why, then?"

She went home trying to act normally, but she could not sleep. She thought, "I did a lot of good work for schools and for all the community. Will I be able to continue doing it if the word goes out? What will my husband think if I tell him? How can I have a good conscience if I hide this from him?"

That night, she sobbed herself to sleep. She felt guilty and wanted to know why she had done this. It had all been humiliating. This punishment hit her on the chin, and she had to learn from it. Her agony prevented her from sleeping. She was lying down watching her husband sleeping in peace while her agony was tormenting her.

Her son was confused too. He did not know if he did the right thing by confronting his mom or not. He did not know if he did the right thing by promising to keep this secret or not. He, too, agonized and could not sleep.

The next day, they met in the parking lot. She was sitting in her car waiting for him, but he was ten minutes late when she saw him leaving his car and going to the store. She called to him, and he came to her.

"Good morning. I came, and I hope you have the papers as you promised," she said.

"Let me just go punch in, and I will be right back with the papers."

He walked away and disappeared into the store. A few minutes later, he showed up with the papers in his hand.

"Here they are."

"Sorry for what had happened."

"You should put this behind you. Who's perfect? You're not perfect. You are just a human being."

"Can I tell you a little story that fits this situation?"

"I'm sorry, Mom. I have to go back to work. I don't want to be seen here after punching in."

He turned and walked away from his mother. As they parted, each one was thinking.

"What kind of lesson did my son take away from this?" she thought.

"What kind of lesson did my mom learn from all this?" he thought.

Flying Down I-94 to My Freedom
Brenda McCall

"I'm free! I'm free! Thank God Almighty! 'I'm Free' has never rung so true! Misery! Don't live here no more!"

That was what I said when I was done with the marriage that had lasted almost twenty years. Ending it released me from the stress, the pain, and the shame. It was truly liberating. The stress was like doing 200 pushups carrying on my back the 2005 Durango truck in which I drove him to Indiana. I gave myself permission and just let go!

After so many years of holding on to something that I knew was cancerous and toxic, I was sure that it was going to be extremely tough and painful to continue. My epiphany was the realization that the man that I had tried to love and care about for over twenty years was never going to change and become the father, husband, or the man I wanted and needed him to be. The first night in MY bed alone without his ASS was empty and counterproductive to what my mind thought and my heart felt! SHIT! SHIT! SHIT! DAMN!

I guess I should start from the beginning. Huh?

I was born in Alabama on October 12, 1966. My mother was not married when she gave birth to me at age seventeen, and later she was nineteen when she gave birth to my asthmatic sister, Debra. I only knew our father, David, when I was a child, though as I became an adult I came to understand more about him. At twenty, my mother married my stepfather, Cleveland, who was twenty years older than she was. She married him to provide stability for her two young daughters and companionship for herself. They found a house on an old country road in a community that was near members of both families. I was three years old when they married, and my sister was one. I don't remember a whole lot of the first years, but I do remember being about four years old, sitting at the dinner table with him telling me to eat my food. The next thing I knew, he held me upside down by my ankles and was beating the shit out of me.

FROM ALABAMA TO HIGHLAND PARK, MICHIGAN

I don't know why my mother left my stepfather, but at five and a half I do remember my mother taping up brown boxes. My mother, brother, sister, and I were boarding a Greyhound Bus going to live with my grandmother in Highland Park, Michigan. Life was really different when we moved in with my grandparents. I had seven cousins who lived downstairs and one only a couple years older who played with me. For the first time in my life, I saw snow, and I had to wear a thick winter coat and boots. When we still lived in Alabama, I ran around barefoot all the time. The only time I ever had to wear shoes was when I went to school or church. Everybody made fun of my country accent and my backward ways. I don't remember when and I don't know why, but one day my stepfather lived with us again. When he moved to Michigan, we eventually moved into the downstairs flat after my cousins moved out.

My stepfather was an abusive alcoholic who drank all day long. He couldn't or wouldn't hold down a full-time job. He drank all day with his neighbor friends while my mother held down two jobs at different nursing homes. For years, my mother left the house at 6:30 in the morning and didn't return home until 11:30 p.m. or midnight. She would wake my siblings and me up and get us dressed and fed before she left. I don't quite understand why his alcoholic aggression seemed to focus on me, but it did. He would pass out on the floor in a drunken stupor after drinking triple shots of Mohawk Vodka from a baby food jar. His alcoholic aggression against me lasted for years. I used to threaten to kill myself or run away because he always seemed to seek me out for whatever alcoholic rage-fueled reason to beat me. I had done nothing wrong for him to treat me in such a way. I still have marks that I can vividly describe how he inflicted them on me. When I was about seven years old, I took refuge in the bathroom closet for hours and I played with my imaginary friend David and his cousins Gino and Robbie and my cousin Mary. When my stepdad started cussing and acting foolishly, I used to hide away to stay out of his reach.

During this time, my relationship with my grandmother started to become my anchor to love and sanity. Besides hiding out, the only other place I had was upstairs, in my grandmother's room. I spent hours with her. She taught me how to cook homemade cakes, pies, and these cookies called Tea Cakes. She taught me to sew and clean house. My grandmother took me with her just about everywhere she went. We'd talk for hours and laugh about anything and everything. When my stepfather called me downstairs to do something, my grandmother would tell me in a reminding tone of voice, "Do it right the first time!"

That meant to do whatever he said: the dishes, the bathroom, the floors, or watching my sisters and brother. That was done correctly and as close to perfection as my nine-year-old body could manage so that he wouldn't have anything to complain or get mad about and I could move myself out of his way as quickly as possible. As soon as I could, I'd hurry back upstairs where my grandmother was. I saw my grandparents as my protectors because my grandfather told him that he would blow his motherf—ing head off if he hit me again. He wouldn't dare to approach those stairs to bother me while my grandfather was at home. My grandfather traveled back and forth to Alabama because he had family and property that he maintained there, but my round-and-robust, five-foot-two grandmother could hold her own. When she walked, she waddled. Her waddle earned her the nickname Duck. She went to church every Sunday morning to praise God. She was the sweetest, most generous, funniest, kindest, and most loving woman I had ever met. She did not take any crap from anybody. She demanded respect from her kids and grandkids. She could be loud and very opinionated when needed.

"I ain't taking shit from no damn body, from the youngest to the oldest. Try me if you want to!" she said in a boisterous and threatening tone of voice that instilled fear in whoever was listening to her. No disrespect was ever displayed around, or to my grandmother. Her grown children never spoke to her loudly or said any profane cuss words in her presence. Whenever she went into her bedroom for her double barrel shot gun, no more explanations were needed.

My grandparents told my mother several times how my stepfather treated me, but she never did or said anything that I know of. I guess she thought that he was a good parent because he didn't do that to my sister Debra. I began to have bad behavior. I got really good at fighting and stealing things: money, toys, clothes, cigarettes, and anything else that I wanted. I stole money and cigarettes from my mother's, aunts', and family friends' purses. When asked if I took the money,

12

of course I lied. I stole from my teacher and classmates. When I was asked if I took it, of course I lied. Whatever I wanted, I just took it! Once, when my class had permission to bring in a toy or game to share with the class, I don't remember if I didn't have a toy to bring or if I just forgot to bring one, but I didn't have anything to share. I was jealous and I did not participate. The teacher coaxed me into playing a board game that one girl brought in to share. I had so much fun playing this game that I plotted how to take it home. While everyone was distracted cleaning up, I smoothly slid the game under my coat. As soon as I got home, I pulled the game out and started playing it with my sister and cousins. When my mother asked me about the game and where I got it from, I told her that my teacher gave it to me. When the game was discovered missing, the teacher called all the students' homes in an effort to locate the game. My mother made me take the game back to the school and apologize to the teacher and my classmate. As I walked back home, I knew that when I got in the house I was going to get my ass torn up. I walked back as slowly as I could, wishing that I could walk slowly backward in the opposite direction.

I started lying and making up stories. Many times there wasn't a need to lie; I just did. I lied on my sisters, brother, and cousins to get them in trouble instead of me. I did it so much that eventually, when they did do stuff, I got in trouble because by then nobody believed me even when I was not at fault.

HIGHLAND PARK TO DETROIT

When I was ten, we moved into another two-family flat, again with my grandparents upstairs. I thought that when we moved everything would change, but nothing changed the patterns in my life. I still hid in closets, still ran upstairs to hang out with my grandmother. I was so stressed out I started to lose my hair. I was, and still am, bald in my temple. Some of what my mother said was true when she told people why my hair fell out on the side. When she used to comb my hair the rubber bands used to be too tight and sometime sores would form, but I was also stressed out from the bad way that I was treated.

My stepfather accused and abused me almost daily. At this point, I actually did some of the things I was accused of doing, but I did not care. It really didn't matter if I did it or not; I still got blamed and beaten. I started to thrive on the bad and negative, mostly for the attention. Some attention was better than no attention. After so many years, somewhere between twelve and thirteen, I stopped caring about what I did. I lost my hair along with my self-esteem and any confidence I had. I had to deal with the mean and relentless teasing of my junior high classmates. All I knew was that I just wasn't loved by my mother. All she seemed to care about was Debra, Man, Myisha, and her two jobs. I had felt misplaced and forgotten for as long as I can remember. It was as if I had to find love wherever I could, and I searched all over. It always seemed as if my mother was mad at me or blamed me for something. To this day I have never known why, but I have my suspicions. All I'm going to say about that is: I wasn't there; I'm just the product of the situation.

Sometimes the subject was put on the table to discuss openly the fact that she had never loved me and why she never gave a damn about me, her first-born child. Of course, she had always denied that my stepfather abused me when the family clearly saw it for themselves. My grandmother confronted my mother at 11:45 p.m., almost as soon as she walked into the house from her second job, about my stepfather beating me

14

because he said that I didn't clean the bathroom good enough. My grandmother told my mother that she waited for my stepfather to leave the house before she came downstairs to check for herself how I cleaned the bathroom. She told my mother that the bathroom was clean and in order. She told her that the sink, tub, and toilet were clean and the floor was mopped.

"What the f—k else does he want her to do?" my grandmother asked my mother. I also heard when my grandmother said, "She cleaned it better than that son of a bitch could ever do!"

"He probably only made her finish cleaning up what she didn't do after he had whooped her. She needed her behind torn up because she is lazy and hardheaded!" my mother retorted. My mother was no dummy; she knew better than to say ass or any other profane language in front of my grandmother.

In 1982, I started high school. I was in the ninth grade when I was fourteen. This should have been a reasonably good time in my life, being in high school. Every week my mother set up an afterschool routine for my siblings and me. Each of us had seven days to clean whatever she assigned: kitchen, bathroom, cleaning the living and dining rooms and vacuuming. We did our homework first, then we ate dinner, cleaned the house, watched television, had bath, and were in bed by 9 p.m. Sometimes after we were all in bed, my drunken stepfather woke me up claiming that I hadn't cleaned whatever job I had that week. He made me clean the area again and also made me clean my siblings' areas too. I went back to bed a few minutes before my mother walked into the house. When my grandmother heard him yelling at me, she made her way downstairs to see what was going on. My grandmother helped me clean up, and then I went upstairs with her for the night. When I was getting ready for school one morning, my baby sister, Myisha, was crying because she wanted cereal for breakfast and not the oatmeal he made. She mistakenly knocked the bowl onto the floor, but instead of him cleaning the floor he called me into the kitchen and made me clean and mop the whole floor. I was late for school that day, and he needed to write a note to excuse the tardiness, but he was drunk already.

I started being really disrespectful to my stepfather because I was tired of being his whipping post. I hated that motherf—er with cold and calculating determination. I started thinking of ways to kill him. I thought about using the old and very heavy iron to bash his skull in as he lay passed out. I thought about dissolving rat poison and pouring it into his liquor bottle. I thought about boiling water on the stove and pouring it down his body from his head to his feet while he was passed out. There were several other very fantastical and imaginative ideas that ran through my head. I felt that I didn't have anything to lose. I felt it was him or me and so I started fighting back. Since I talked to my grandmother about everything, I told her about my murder plan. I explained to her all about the ways I was planning to send his ass to hell. That day I'm not sure whose life my grandmother saved, his or mine. She begged me! She said with tears in her eyes, "Babe don't do it. He ain't worth you spending the rest of your life in prison." She told me about a time when my grandfather spent ten years in prison for killing a man in self-defense. After that conversation, I did consider suicide for few days, but I wasn't willing to hurt my grandmother by leaving this life. I did not want to hurt the only person who loved me, because I wasn't sure if my mother would have given a damn.

He started drinking before sun up and passed out just as the last drop of alcohol would slide through the neck of the bottle. God only knows what he drank during the day, but just

16

as he had sucked down his last pint of Mohawk Vodka and passed out, you could literally see as piss stained the front of his pants. When he woke up looking for the bottle and found it empty, he accused me of pouring it out and then he started hitting me. I could feel the welts as they rose up on my skin as he hit me with a doubled-up extension cord. I was trying to stave off the licks of the old brown electrical cord with my stretched-out hands. He did not care where the licks landed: my head, my legs, my arms, my back, or my face. One blow caused a large blood blister to form on the palm of my right hand. The blister was the size of a ping pong ball. I could not hold a pencil to write or hold silverware to eat with my right hand for a whole week. To this day I still have it as a reminder: a small faded brown mark on the palm of my hand. After that, I decided that I just wasn't taking that shit anymore. Every time after that, whenever he tried to hit me, I fought back. With him being really drunk and unsteady on his feet, I would kick, punch, and if I got close enough, I would even bite him. I sent a loud and clear message that I wasn't going to take it anymore and I was standing up for myself.

Once, when he tried to hit me, I socked him in the jaw, and then he tried to grab me. I kicked him, and he fell backward into the china cabinet. I took off running into the bathroom, locked the door, and stayed in there until my mother came home. She made me unlock and open the door. As my mother pulled to open the door wider, my stepfather threw a shoe so hard that when it hit me above my left eye blood instantly gushed out. I thought that my eye was busted and apparently so did my mother because when she turned around she started to beat the hell out of him. She punched him so hard he stumbled backward, almost falling. Then he started trying to hit my mother. That was when my sister Debra grabbed the mop,

17

beating him upside the head. By then I realized that my eye was fine. The three of us jumped on him, and the fight was on. We beat his ass from the back of the house to the living room in the front. Somehow, my sister was still hitting him with the mop handle. I don't remember how long it took, but by the end of the month my step father was back in Alabama.

FREED FROM DRAMA AND ABUSE, SO I THOUGHT

By the time I was fifteen and in tenth grade, my mother divorced my stepfather. She continued to work two jobs at different nursing homes. My mother started to date the car mechanic, Red, who eventually moved in with us. It seemed as though my mother found yet another person to put in front of me. I tried to ignore Red with every fiber of my being, but he always had some type of drama going in our house. Red always favored my younger siblings, Myisha and Cleveland (Man). My sister Debra and I didn't really care for him. Red was able to influence my mother in a way that my stepfather could not. Once, she and I went to the furniture store to buy four beds for my siblings and me. For a change, I had all of my mother's attention. We had so much fun being silly and goofy lying down and bouncing on the different beds. I picked out my set and helped her pick out the others. Come the day of delivery, I was very excited to get my new set in my room. I woke two hours before I usually got up for school. I moved the broken down old bed, dresser, and chest piece by piece into the dumpsters. After I finished, I got cleaned up and went to school. I was fidgety throughout the school day and I couldn't wait until school was out. Finally, school was out, and I was not going to wait on the slow city bus to show up. I made my sister Debra walk the sixteen blocks home and she complained all the way, but she was excited too. When we got home all the boxes from all our new furniture were on the front porch. Debra and I rushed into the house to our rooms to see our new beds. I said in my mind, "What the f—k?"

"Where is my shit?" I yelled for my mother. She was in her room. When I opened her door, my brand new bedroom was set up in her room. She let Red convince her to take my new bedroom set. He told her that the bedroom set was much to grown up for me. So they put my new bed, dresser, and chest in her bedroom and they put all the old used shit out of her room into mine. I was so mad and hurt; I couldn't believe that she would do that to me. She knew how much I loved and wanted that set. Red really found the whole situation hilarious. He'd make snide comments or he'd ask me if I liked my new bedroom set. The whole time that I was crying and pleading with my mother to put my new bed in my room, he was laughing. I started to really hate that motherf—er from then on. I pleaded with my mother for weeks to put my new bed in my room. Red would tell my mother that I did or didn't do something, just to hear her yell, cuss me out, or hit me, while he stood on the side line being entertained and laughing. One day, while he was laughing at me because my mother was fussing, as I brushed past him I jumped up and stomped down on his foot so hard I hoped that it broke. He yelped very loud as he grabbed at his foot, but the motherf—er wasn't laughing anymore. I heard my mother yelling behind me, "Why you do that? You know that he's diabetic!"

"I hope gangrene eats up the whole motherf—ing leg up to his ass bone," I yelled back at both of them before I ran out the house and caught the bus to my Cousin Mary's house.

By this time, I had been through many years of abuse and I was not going to deal with anybody else getting a turn. As we got older, our daily routine had relaxed a little bit. When we got home, we chilled out and did whatever we wanted just as long as everything was done before my mother got home. The real reason that we waited so late to clean up was because somebody always messed up something. So we figured why clean up twice when we could clean everything just before we went to bed. It would still be clean when my mother walked through the door. Usually, around 10:00 p.m., we would have everything done.

One day Red decided that he would make us clean up the house about 5:00 p.m., and I told him that it was not time for us to clean up yet. He pulled off his belt and hit me. I jumped up and said to him, "If you ever f—ing hit me again, mama is going to wake up next to a corpse. I'm going to take the iron and bash your motherf—ing head in while you asleep!" Of course he told my mother what I had said when she got home. When my mother called me into her room, she asked me what I had said to Red. Looking her straight in the eye, without stuttering or blinking, I repeated what I told him word for word. I reiterated that if he ever hit me again, she would wake up next to a corpse because I was going to take the iron and bash his motherf—ing head while he was asleep. She was shocked and waved me away with dumbfounded silence. Red never came at me like that again, but he would try to instigate drama between my boyfriend David and me. He would make supposedly innocent comments to David. While he was laughing, he said things to make David believe that I was cheating. After one of Red's poisonous insinuations, I said to him, "Next time you go into diabetic shock, I'm going to slip some rat poison dust into your sugar cocktail if you keep on f—ing with me."

He knew that I could do it because if my mother wasn't home, I was the only one who knew how to mix up the concoction for him. After that threat, he never bothered me again.

DOING MY OWN THING

I went to school, but I learned how to skip in the tenth grade. I wasn't skipping and going to other people's houses when their parents weren't home. I heard crazy stories about girls hanging out at houses with guys using drugs and having trains run on them. A train is when multiple guys line up to have sex with one female. "Watch what happens to these girls before you try what they do," my neighbor always warned me. I stayed away from the street life. I went home to watch the game shows and soap operas and I would hide in my old sanctuary, the closet, when I heard my grandmother coming down the stairs. When I did hang out, I was with my cousin. She would pick me up around the corner from my house, and we hung out all day. Then she would drop me off in the same spot when school was over, so I could walk home as if I was at school all day.

I started drinking and smoking weed in eleventh grade. I only drank and smoked weed with people that I knew, because I trusted them. After a couple of bad experiences with smoking weed, I left it alone because it made me higher than liquor ever did. I was offered cocaine, but since I didn't like the effects that the weed had on me, I figured cocaine would be the same way. I drank liquor when I hung out, usually with my cousin and best friend.

Throughout the years, I dated several guys who were named David. It seemed as if every David in Detroit and the surrounding areas was looking for me, and I found them. Each one came with his own version of craziness. My boyfriends weren't all named David, but there were more Davids than statistically normal. I found refuge in different guys. I guess I was looking for some kind of love, protection, and attention. During my quest for attention and security, I became pregnant several times resulting in abortions. My first pregnancy was a few weeks before my sixteenth birthday. I went to visit my aunt in Saginaw, Michigan for the summer. Over in the projects by the railroad tracks, in Saginaw, Michigan, I was bored out of my mind. I had nothing to do but watch the trains go by all day. The store closed early at 6:00 p.m. and didn't open at all on Saturday and Sunday. I wanted to entertain myself. When I saw my type, light, bright next to a white cutie walking down the block, I started flirting with him. His name was Darin, not David, but close enough! He lived with his grandmother in the same projects down the street. After that first meeting, we hung out every day, either at my aunt's apartment or at his grandmother's apartment. Other than the little kissing, touching, and feeling, nothing serious ever happened because we were both virgins. One day, when his grandmother wasn't at home, the touching and feeling got way out of hand at his grandmother's house. Until this day, I'm not sure he ever figured out how to put it in. There was a lot of grunting, sweating, and anxiousness. I remember thinking, "Was that how 'it' was supposed to be?" Seemed like a lot of dry humping to me, nothing special.

About six weeks later, I was on an exam table in the abortion clinic. I told Darin afterwards. Just like me, he was relieved. My mother tried to convince me to keep the baby, but I was determined not to be like her. I was just sixteen. She had me at seventeen, and I resented it my whole life. After calling me several choice names my mother took me the first and second times. The other two times I used my cousin's state Medicaid card for the abortions. I have been regretting it with guilt every day since. I remember the faces, I remember the conversations, I remember the smell, and most of all I remember the way the vacuum machine sounded as it sucked my baby out of me. It gave a loud slurping, slurping, and slurping and then something was stuck or the hose was clogged. The feelings of emptiness, shame, guilt, and loss consumed me! I was overwhelmed by all of these feelings. These feelings never went away after that! They were ingrained in the depth of my soul, yet I did it again and again and again!

LOSING TWO PARTS OF MY SOUL

In 1990, I lost my anchor to love: my grandmother died. When she died, it was like an ocean liner pulling up her anchor and sailing away to the next port. Diagnosed with Pancreatic Cancer in July and gone on October 24, I saw her chain, the links representing each year of her life, pulling up the anchor with news of the cancer. She began to slowly move forward with the prognosis. Realizing there was nothing more the doctors could do, I knew that my grandmother was going to die. She wouldn't be here much longer, and time was racing and speeding in the sterile hospital room with all the beeping machines. I saw her moving faster as the doctors were reading her charts, nurses administered pain medicines through the IV, preachers praying and quoting scriptures, and the family crying and begging God not to take her just yet. I started chasing and calling to her, "Please don't leave me." Knowing that she was suffering, I felt guilty asking her to stay. When the doctor pronounced her passing, suddenly I couldn't breathe, my pulse slowed, I fainted to the floor. My best friend, my mother, and my grandmother was gone. I could not process the thought and make myself believe that she was gone forever; I was numb.

One year later, 1991, on an icy Christmas Eve, my twenty-three-year-old sister Debra was leaving for work. She asked my mother to let her out of the driveway. My mother went out to back her car out so my sister could leave, but they forgot that Branden, one year old, could open the front door. They asked me to watch him, but I was so tired because we had been out for hours, shopping. Therefore, my mother told Debra to go up on the porch with Branden until she parked on the street and then she would come and get him. Debra got out of her car and proceeded to walk around behind my mother's car to the porch. As she rounded the rear of the car, it slid on some black ice. My mother tried to hit the brakes but instead she hit the gas. The car flew backward hitting my sister, and rolling her body under the car from the back passenger side of the car to the front driver's side. The car stopped across the street in the neighbor's driveway with the tire resting on my sister's body. With adrenaline pumping through their bodies, my boyfriend David and several other men actually hoisted the car up off the ground and moved it away from my sister. She was alive, thank God. At the hospital, we found out that she was going to survive. Debra never lost consciousness throughout the accident. Both of her front teeth, her shoulder, one leg, and her pelvis were broken. She needed to have surgery to place pins into her shoulder, leg, and pelvis. Since it was Christmas and New Year's holidays, most of the surgical teams were on vacation. Debra had to wait until a few days after the New Year to receive the surgery.

As she lay down waiting, the nursing staff administered pain medicines and blood thinners. When doctors administered medicine, they used the person's weight to determine the

24

dosage. Debra was in the hospital for a week and a half waiting to have the surgery. Since she weighed about two hundred and twenty pounds, the proper amount of blood thinner medicine was not administered. While she lay there waiting, her body formed blood clots. The day of the surgery finally was scheduled for 7:00 a.m. She called my mother and me, and we rushed to the hospital before they took her to surgery. We made it about ten minutes before they took her down. We told her that we loved her and we would see her in the recovery room. The nurse predicted the surgery would last about four to five hours.

After they took her down, my mother and I went into the surgical lounge to wait. Since the surgery was supposed to last four to five hours, my mother decided that we would go pay the water bill. I dropped her off at the door and drove around until she came out. We were gone for about an hour. When we walked back to the surgical lounge, all hell broke loose. While we were gone, the hospital staff had been paging us because something went seriously wrong with my sister. When they administered the anesthesia and her body became relaxed, several blood clots dislodged and traveled through her body. Of the two clots in her lungs, one lodged in her heart causing a heart attack and through all the chatter of the doctors, I believe they said one was in her brain, causing her to have a stroke. She lay in the surgical intensive care unit for a week. My mother spent the whole week at the hospital, not sleeping or eating. From the lack of sleep, my mother's eyes turned blood red with no white to be seen. My twenty-three-year-old sister was never to wake up again. She slipped away leaving Branden and the rest of us behind. Until this day, I blame myself for my sister's death. "If only I had gotten up to get Branden," I say to myself.

25

JANUARY 4, 1994

After five years of dating and a daughter, I married David in Toledo, Ohio at the Justice of the Peace. We started dating in November 1989, and we spent every free moment together. From the beginning, our relationship had some ups and downs. Love is blind, deaf, and stupid. Love made me look over and past almost anything. We argued, cussed, and called each other all types of names, but we always made up and we never went to bed mad. Our relationship grew for two years before we had our first daughter, Gabrielle. He moved in with me while I was pregnant. He always had some sort of job and tried to take care of us the best he could. He was paid, at the most, minimum wage on any of his jobs. He went to school for interior communication to learn how to install telephones and cable power lines. After one of our many arguments, I told him to get the hell out. He moved out and back in with his mother and sister. Of course, they made their judgments based on his side of the story.

In July 1993, he told me that he had enlisted in the Navy. That day was very surreal. It was the day that I really knew and understood that I was crazy in love with this man. I felt a sense of loss and separation and I didn't want him to leave. I thought that we were going to break up for good that time. Each of us had caused our share of the pain, misery, and hurt. In reality, I really wouldn't have blamed him if he had turned his back and forgotten that I existed. Early on, after Gabrielle was born, he was very insecure. He didn't believe that he fathered her, because my mother's boyfriend Red instigated drama. I told David, "Call me if you ever wanted to take a paternity test at any time or place." It certainly was no Immaculate Conception, so I wasn't concerned about who had fathered

26

my daughter. I also told him that if he insisted on a paternity test and the test proved him the father, he should send the check and never call. David loved his daughter very much, and he called every day to check on her.

When he left for Boot Camp, I didn't hear from him for two weeks. I learned later that the military had a policy that new recruits only got one five-minute phone call informing families of their arrival on the base. He called his mother and sister, but I had to wait the time out. About a week after he left I received a letter from him explaining why he didn't call me when he got on the base. We wrote to each other every week, even after the two-week cock block, and he called me whenever he got a leave. We planned for me to come to his Boot Camp graduation in Great Lakes Illinois. His six weeks of boot camp was up in early December, and he came home for a thirty day leave. We were married three days before he was to report for duty in San Diego, California on January 4, 1994.

My first time to ever fly in an airplane was three months after we were married. During the three months of waiting, my excitement grew to the size of an airplane. I packed up everything in the house because the Navy was sending a moving company truck to ship our belongings to San Diego. When the day of our flight finally came, I was so nervous and petrified that I could hardly function. The thought of going on a plane terrified the shit out of me. What happened to all the gung ho bravado? At the airport, I tried to calm down. My nerves had me hyperventilating and sweating. When they called for boarding passes, I panicked as I walked toward the passenger tunnel. I told my mother that I wasn't going. I turned around and headed for the moving side walk. My mother caught me and literally pushed me to the plane just as they were about to close the door. I stood there crying and watching my mother cry as the door closed. I never prayed so hard in my life. I recited Matthew 6:9 for the entire four hours.

Thank God, it was a straight flight with no stop overs or switching plane connections.

Gabrielle and I landed in San Diego to start our new lives as military dependents. I grew up fast because I didn't have anybody to depend on except my husband. Life in San Diego was an adjustment process, and it took a few weeks to settle in. The hardest adjustment was when my husband left for the first weeks or a month on a naval cruise. When it came time for him to leave on a Western Pacific cruise (West Pac) for six months, I panicked and flew home to Detroit for five of the six months. Six months with a small child and without my husband in a city that I had no real knowledge of and having no family or friends terrified me. We didn't have a car so I had to learn how to navigate the city buses and trolley. I had to take the bus to the trolley station and the trolley to the military base so I could shop for groceries. I had to learn where to find the doctors' offices and the hospital. Gabrielle had asthma and was sick regularly. I eventually settled, learned, and adjusted to almost everything except for staying in San Diego when David left on the many West Pac cruises. When that happened, I always came back to Detroit. We were enlisted for eight years, and while he traveled the world, I maintained the home front.

When David would return home from West Pac, we were happy and relieved. It was as if I got a new husband for a couple of weeks. While he was away, I only had only Gabrielle, and she only had me. Gabrielle and I did everything together. We had an everyday routine and stability. I took care of her, and she depended solely on me. When David came home, Gabrielle, being so young, didn't understand why she had to obey her father. Every time he told her to do anything she would always ask me if it was okay. David took offence at her asking me before she did what he asked her. This behavior set the tone for their relationship for years to come. Being the oldest of four kids and the victim of abuse, I tried to explain to David the importance of constant stability to a child. He had to work, and unfortunately his job required him to be away from home regularly. I tried to get him to understand that Gabrielle gravitated to me because I was there every day. He loved her, but David held this resentment and ultimately it caused damage that resulted in years of unnecessary pain and hurt to his daughter.

HONORABLY DISCHARGED

Our problems started as David became more and more irritated by the separations and the command authority. When the ship's new commanding officer took command of the USS Comstock, he seemed to focus his primary attention on the interior communication department. He made several changes and demotions. David wasn't demoted, but he was reprimanded for something that he didn't feel was justified. After several other situations, David became more disconnected and started a downward spiral. David had an uncanny ability to sabotage his own life, and sometimes he was his own worst enemy. I don't think that David understood consequences. He would run full steam into a brick wall, and then he would complain of a headache. Consciously or unconsciously, David had demolished our lives many times and in many ways. Regardless of the consequences, or who was affected, he did whatever he wanted. David knew the military had a weight standard, along with a physical agility qualifying test every year. He failed one of the tests because he didn't meet the weight requirement. The military installed him in a mandatory weight loss program, where he had six months to come within the weight standard and complete the physical training. Everything that the doctor suggested, David did the opposite. He drank alcohol, ate fried food, and did not exercise unless he was under supervision on the ship. He failed the physical again and was honorably discharged. Here was the demolition of our lives.

FROM SAN DIEGO TO DETROIT

When we moved back to Detroit, things were okay as we were adjusting to being back home. In this process, we found out that I was pregnant. This pregnancy ended in a second miscarriage. Soon after that, David had a job working for Rent-A-Center as manager, and I found out that I was pregnant again. Makaila was born July 31, 2000. When Makaila was born, David seemed to turn his back on Gabrielle altogether. Gabrielle started to ask why her daddy hated her. I started to see old patterns from my early life. Instead of the mother-daughter, it was the father-daughter broken relationship. I was the referee between them, always trying to keep the peace. David and I were both the product of missing biological fathers. In an effort to give our daughters the stability of two biological parents who raised them together, I never really considered leaving.

SPIRALING DOWN

David eventually got a job at work for Ameritech installing phone and cable lines. He was making over twenty dollars an hour. Our lives should have greatly improved because he was making enough money to pay all our bills, keep food in the house, and to buy whatever we wanted. Instead of taking care of his family, however, David became stingy, mean, and hateful. His take-home pay was over twenty-five hundred dollars biweekly. He wouldn't deposit any money in the bank account. He took his entire paycheck to work with him because he did not want me to spend any. Our bills got even further behind because he only paid a portion each month. I had to almost beg for money and open myself up to a barrage of hateful insults. Usually, when he gave me money, I would spend it on things needed for the kids, the house, and even for him. I never spent much, if any, on myself unless I truly needed to. When I asked for money to pay bills, I opened myself up to even more hateful insults. I stopped asking for the most menial things that I needed, such as maxi pads, soap, and deodorant. I was beat and broke down, mentally and emotionally. I was dependent on David. The only bright spot in my life at that time was my babies.

During our marriage, my already low self-esteem reached the point of non-existence. I cried almost every day because I could not understand why he treated me so badly. The disrespect and hate that he had for me broke my spirit. The usually happy-go-lucky person had died in me, and I hadn't even noticed. He never wanted me to get a job. He said that Makaila was too young to go to day care. I agreed and dropped the subject, until one day while he was at work, I went to a job fair and was hired at Technicolor. I waited until three days before my orientation to tell him, and that was only because I needed the car to get there. I worked for Technicolor ten and half years, and during this time David lost the Ameritech job and at least seven others. Self-destruction was the main area that he specialized in. When he lost a job, the average time to the next one ranged from one to two years. The one job that I had, the one he forbade me to have, carried us through hard times.

Through the many years of my working, the tables turned in several ways. I became the provider of our household; I paid all the bills, brought all the food, and took care of the kids. When I left at 4:30 a.m., he was asleep. When I got home at 3:00 p.m., he was asleep. I never really had a problem with him being at home if only he took care of house and home. If he couldn't work, at least he could have taken care of the house and his family in another way. But we weren't his main priority. When I was home, I cooked, cleaned the house, and washed everybody's clothes. When he was working, I was always up before he left for work. He did none of these things at the time I worked and he stayed home! He wouldn't cook unless it was just for himself at 10:00 p.m. He never cleaned or washed anything. He lay around the house and played video games. He had a sense of entitlement as if I owed him something. The more time passed, the more I worked, and the more I took on the roles of the mother and father both to him and to our kids.

A SEED IS PLANTED

A light wind blew, shaking a rejected seed from the tree of hopelessness, misery, pain, despair, desolation, anguish, gloom, depression, despondency, dejection, and unhappiness. Like me, the seed landed on the ground with barely a thud, not noticed by anyone. Like me, the seed planted itself among the debris, and started to grow. As my roots became stronger, I grew mentally and emotionally. I wasn't a victim of the tree anymore. I wasn't the same person seeking love and acceptance from those who do not have love or willingness to accept anyone besides themselves. Something had changed within me. I found love and acceptance within myself. I found within myself the strength to stand up and be a real woman. I hadn't noticed the change, but I had survived the deaths of my mother, stepfather, grandmother, and my sister. I was no longer the meek and submissive shell. I finally realized that I existed in a place and space where only I resided. I became responsible for my own happiness, and I didn't need to play the blame game anymore. My search for acceptance was to find it within myself. With this revelation, I understood what I had been searching for. I needed security and protection from the storm. I needed a safe harbor to rest. I just wanted what every other child wanted and I sought that safe harbor in anyone that showed me a tiny bit. I made that my life and planted roots, even though they didn't go very deep.

I could do badly by myself, and I had been standing on my own for years, time for a change. I couldn't put up with the status quo. I was fed up and I could not deal with his trifling ass anymore. It was time that David and I called it quits and ended the cycle of unhappiness. He decided to move out of state to Indianapolis, Indiana, the place of his birth. As he packed his belongings, I was secretly giddy inside. I walked around with a smirk on my face, and when he couldn't rent a U-Haul truck I volunteered to take him. David packed up my 2005 Durango truck so full that I couldn't even see out the rear window. On I-94, I drove the five hour trip with Makaila, Lisa, David, me, and all of David's shit. We arrived in Indianapolis around 3:00 p.m. and unpacked all his stuff. We stayed for about an hour before leaving to return home the same day. I was a little sad, and Makaila cried, but I was done with the marriage that had lasted almost twenty years. The road between David and home allowed me to be released from the stress, the pain, and the shame. It was truly liberating.

I gave myself permission to relax and just let go! I thought, "Misery! Don't live here no more!"

Little White Pieces of What

Peter Raymond Agar II

PART ONE . . .

I collapsed alone in the playground at a post-apocalyptic setting in my elementary school. My legs gave out as moist noodles pushed through boiling hot water. Around me were broken swings and a dead tree. Both played parts in each other's demise. The tree grew partly under the metal swing, which eventually caused it to fall on the other side due to its poor foundation. My mouth felt as if I was chewing on sandpaper, and my body was shaking uncontrollably. I sat up straight and tried to maintain that posture but I felt I was like a washing machine with an unbalanced load. I needed sugar lest I pass out. I reached into my coat pocket to eat the liquorish I was saving from lunch. The grass was wet and was uncomfortable under my jeans. It was the beginning of March. The air was cold. The wind pushed my eyes closed, but I was too woozy to keep them shut. Every time I shut them, I got tingles in the back of my thighs. This brought the sensation of falling from an extreme height. I was scared. I felt like this from time to time. The wind stopped. How peculiar the world looked at that particular time! It was 40 degrees, but I felt like I was in the Sahara. Eager exhaustion came to me in waves, and I started focusing on the sun. The wind and clouds stood serene. The only movement was the heat waves brought on by staring at the sun and low blood sugar that gave me this deceitful mirage. I caught a glimpse of a shadowy figure in the distance through the waves as if it was walking through fire. It was clearly a man. He was tall and relatively thin. He paced back and forth, clicking his heels to the sidewalk in a sort of retrospective stroll that he took as he reexamined his life. A young boy in my class ran to my aid and disrupted my vision.

Later in the day, we were brought into the gymnasium for a meet-and-greet assembly. It was career day. I panned the enormous room scanning the youthful smiles to the empty beaten-by-life guests that came to recruit the children to sign away their life to bonds, barracks, burgers, and bullshit. I wasn't hungry for this atmosphere. It made me irritable and I was still shaking. I gazed out the gym window and at the open parking lot. I was entranced in the lives of the silent conversation I observed by the grownups cuddling their coffees under their chins. I began to observe a man in his mid-twenties pacing along the parking lot dividers and hopping from one stone to another. I concluded that this man was the shadowy figure and he was real. I studied his face and made assumptions about his personality.

He wore dark pants rolled slightly to see his socks. The pain in his face seemed as if it was painted with a surrealist view of the world, kind of how an art appreciator looked at Leonardo da Vinci pieces, only in everyday life. Nevertheless, he did so with a pessimistic view, a jaded look on the human race. His eyes never seemed to be open all the way, and underneath them were dark circles and hints of red flushed to his cheeks. His fingernails were dirty, and the combat boots he wore looked like they held dirt from every continent. He had seen better days. His hair was blonde and greasy—greasy or damp, I couldn't tell. His eyes remained focused on his own oblivion as he wondered like a steam locomotive engine and studied himself as he chain-smoked cigarette after cigarette. I started to question myself, "Why did I understand this man without ever meeting him formally?" I even knew without seeing that he put his hand in his jacket pocket because he was twirling a loose strand of string hanging out of the stitching. His darkness was burned into my retina. I saw him laughing everywhere I looked. This man had all the powers of hell in his command. When I thought about him that night, I was horrified. I had the kind of terror that sent chills up my spine and scraped the marrow off my bones. Why did I find him so scary? In reality, he wasn't real. He was an illusion or an apparition of my future. He was me, years later, taunting me with my failed destiny.

Ever since that day, I always went against the grain. I never tried to be too overzealous or too timid. After all, they say that we can often meet our destiny on the path we choose to avoid it. Therefore, I study life piece by piece and I learn what I can. I keep my eyes open to opportunity, but never walk backwards too far into the unknown. It's the best I can do. As I grow up, I see the man I viewed in my vision, but with less scars. I believed I was on the right path, but life never comes in clear bold print instructions.

It began the next year in my Catholic school when I truly realized how different I was from every child of my age. My mother had to work two jobs to keep me in that Catholic school. My uniform smelled of the Salvation Army. My shoes were always two sizes too big every time they were new. My mother told me I would grow into them. I spent entire lunches sitting in the cafeteria drawing. Around me were all the girls of my grade waiting for their portraits. They reimbursed me with cookies, candy, or money. They called me their boyfriend, but I was scared to talk to them. This lasted only a few years. Suddenly, the entire seventh grade was a slew of testosterone and emotions. The boys no longer liked me due to my popularity among the female middle school population. I hid from the word "love," the boys and girls I liked were moving on. To these boys, heartbreak was like death. Even at age thirteen. I walked through the halls as if middle school was an alien planet inhabited by emotional, clingy creatures that bled uncontrollably. I lost most of my portrait clientele.

High school wasn't any better. Teenagers were off discovering each other's bodies. I was discovering weed, cigarettes, and eating pizza with ranch. I was one hundred fifteen pounds at fourteen and close to six feet tall. My hair was a mood ring. It carried all kinds of pain from hardship to heartbreak. I changed my appearance. Hair was the only immortal thing in me. I cut it all I wanted, and it still grew. It died but it was still living. I rode my skateboard from city to city collecting memories and street signs, mostly street signs. I rode so hard my right thigh could snap a baseball bat. My diet consisted of junk food, alcohol, and any other unhealthy shit I could get my hands on. My intake of near toxic-vile fast food shit somehow balanced out with my high metabolism and ability to ride a skateboard for ten hours.

THE CATACLYSM OF YELLOW AND GREY . . .

Somewhere along this path to self-destruction, I hit a speed bump, both physically and figuratively. I flew across an asphalt ocean and didn't swim. Instead, I hit the pavement and skipped with my shoulder blades. The road was as unforgiving as a southern judge with marital problems. What could be worse than falling off a skateboard fast, really fast? Falling off a skateboard really fast while going downhill. The cement flashed its penmanship to me by writing its name on my body in my own blood in scattered cursive. My back and legs looked like the bruised strawberries that nobody wanted. After my fall, my heart beat in the strangest way as I laid in the oasis of chewed ground and stone. I slowly felt my freed Indian-like spirit dance away as the breeze carried it off to the beat of a Cherokee skin drum. I laid in the wake of empty consciousness; I bathed in pain, not yet aware of it. I was saddened by the mutiny that God and my guardian angels brought on me. My legs gave way on my hubris throne, and I fell into the abyss with the dirt and worms. I limped for months, but my spirit was already a vegetable. I was poor, from a broken family, and I didn't get along with most people. It was always like this. Only this time I didn't have a sin. For the first time in my life, I was forced to see who I was. I didn't like looking in the mirror. I saw too much of the shadowy figure I had envisioned. Was this some sort of a self-fulfilling prophecy that I was subconsciously carrying out on the path I thought I was taking in order to avoid it? The rhetorical conversations I held with myself meant nothing. I was lost in depression. I continued a vicious path of destroying my body and my spirit with no motive but blind, hapless ambition. My mother always said, "It's the artist's curse. A hundred thread count of isolation and emptiness caught in the fringe. Though it may not seem that way now, but consider yourself lucky." She sometimes found a way with words.

Exit the spirit and enter Tonka stage to the left. Now in the mists of my darkness, aka the twelfth grade, I spent most of my time with a twenty-three-year-old named Tonka. Tonka was six feet and whatever, had a shaved head, and wore a collar of poorly drawn tattoos around his neck. He dropped out of high school but he was smart, too smart actually. There were times when he would come up with bad ideas and I just couldn't tell the difference. He was nice to strangers, but their return glances were replaced with jaded looks. Tonka felt he looked like a skinhead. He had alopecia. He wore his baldness well and he was confident but quiet. He even had a way with women that I never had.

When I first met him, he had been known as Tonka for years. There were many rumors about where the name came from. One of them was that when he was a baby his mother, who was a schizophrenic, rolled him down the road in a toy Tonka truck and he survived. You could tell from his sighs that he was never happy. He felt too much and knew too little of the irresistible sweetness a woman carried when she whispered the words, "I love you!" He knew no greater high. His eyes were always like rainy windowsills. He sometimes was too painful to look at. On weekends, we compared scars. They were our currency of respect amongst our group. Weakness was our blood oath to each other. We were all f—k ups. At least we kept each other company.

At this time of our high school career, hipsters, a cultivated group of upper middle class parasites rejecting their hosts, were on the rise. They had the money and they didn't mind spending copious amounts to make it seem like they didn't care. They wore rags and felt ironic, and we wore the same and felt iconic. We were mistaken so many times. They were pretentious wannabes with nothing better to do but spend their fathers' money and taint my taste in music. They were everywhere in Detroit. My hometown was a cesspool of artists with more talk than talent, girls who fought like men, and men who dressed like women. It was time Tonka and I set out like Lewis & Clark in all our angst.

That evening we lay on the hood of my '92 Saturn as we wallowed in self-pity for the umpteenth time and shared

40

stolen cigarettes. They always tasted sweeter. The wheels of each tire sunk into soft mud on all corners. Only the empty night air and crickets filled the gaps of our conversation like soft white noise. This was peace, but we both had burdens on our shoulders. We masked our aggression with heavy sighs as we talked, and I stared at the stars and the treetops. I carried on rubbing my hands on my face as if things were going to change. Every couple of seconds of doing so, I accumulated a small amount of tears. It was due to rubbing too hard, not from sadness. I liked the way it felt. I forgot how to cry a long time ago. I put my hands under the small of my back to warm them. Tonka dropped the ash on his way to flick the remainder. We were stoned to a level of stupidity and subconscious brilliance. His mellow vibe was quickly interrupted by the burning ember. I stayed back and laughed to myself as he scurried to stop the ember from burning a hole. I remember the vivid view of his side profile as he rolled the ashes of his shirt with the palm of his hand. The exposed annoyed expression on the side of his face faded into an open stare into the woods. He was thinking. I didn't want him to get hurt. After all, he only made it to the tenth grade. It was as if an angel came down riding a lightning bolt crafted on pure adrenalin.

The night fell still as he turned his head to me. The crickets crossed their legs in anticipation. In his eyes was a sure answer to our prayers. He smirked a little and released a faint whisper. In his words, his voice carried the melody of angels as I heard him say, "Dude, let's run away to California." I was blinded by imagination. He had a vocabulary of like sixty-seven words, but that one phrase sounded something like James Joyce's "Little white pieces of what." I muttered out softly.

"What being a noun, here," I explained. I had his attention. "What being wonder, open possibility," I added. "The little white pieces are little life lessons that make us wonder on what. Sometimes I don't even know what I'm saying from time to time. But it felt good to think out loud."

Tonka smiled in a somewhat strange understanding.

"I like that," he whispered.

The next day we had the plan and the day after we had the money. I spent a week returning bottles for change, stealing fifths of Jameson, and selling them to kids my age. In the next week, I opened my tin batman lunch box. It was filled with cigarettes, empty dime bags, a mint green–handled stiletto switchblade, and money I collected since I was ten. I put every dime I had into one pile as I kneeled at the end of my bed. Fourteen hundred dollars were staring back at me. I was a dangerous man. The plan was simple: Carlsbad, CA was 33 hours away. We would stop in Washington City to stay with Tonka's cousin; he was a business opportunist. He wanted to offer us cash and life lessons and was interested in going to California. I'd tell my mom I was staying the night with an imaginary classmate named Mike. Wednesday, Thursday, and Friday were senior skip days, which was also a lie. There really was no school Monday, so I told her I was staying the weekend. We figured that by the time my mom found out I wasn't coming home we'd be in Washington, long gone with no traces. It had been only seventeen years but I already f—ed up so far at this point, I could begin a new life.

LOVE, PEACE & CHICKEN GREASE

It was 7:30 in the morning. My bags were packed. I wore a camouflage T-shirt and a fresh pair of stolen skinny jeans. My combat boot was strapped to attack. I had my Mother

F— suitcase (a suitcase I found on the highway with the initials "M.F." engraved), three packs of cigarettes, and a pint of Canadian whiskey in a cold flask. I met up with Tonka in the school parking lot. We had on the same pair of Lennon sunglasses. Neither of us noticed then how cliché our personas appeared. I parked my car in an abandoned house behind the school and locked the keys inside. Here was the journey ahead. Tonka bought a car for this special journey. It was a 1988 orange-red Volvo station wagon with gnomes on the dash. So there it was, our own personal Mayflower. I slapped on an "I Lift Detroit in Prayer" bumper sticker and we christened it with moonshine from a mayonnaise jar. The car had its name, "Bartleby" after the bohemian short story by Herman Melville. In some weird way, I always felt a connection to Melville. I read about his life here and there. He died at the age of 72 with most people not even knowing who he was. We set out on the road going into Indiana in what seemed to be only a few short hours. Tonka was from Indiana. I had my phone plugged in to the cassette adapter, and we listened to Motown and Doo-wop. For most of the ride, we were honking at beautiful girls, getting gas, and peeing on the side of the highway. There was a lot of time in between our antics when we didn't even say a word to each other. It was our time to stare out on the open road and think about life. I thought about my mother and how I would be eighteen in California. I'd let her know I was alive. Soon enough I could send her money. I'd make everyone proud. They didn't understand me, but soon enough they will. I thought about the girl I left behind. Well, she left me the experience, but my heart was in a George Foreman Grill. Why did I have to love someone who didn't love me? Why did I have to be so different? If I could just kiss her one more time, if I could just tell her "I love you" one more time. I want her to speak my name or for me to

43

fall out of love so that I could listen to music and not think of her. In every awkward encounter I had seen her after we broke up, I wanted to feel her lips against mine and sob as I had done before. She made me feel something I never felt before. I felt lovable, somewhat normal. That night, I lay cradled in the back of our road-trip wagon under the moonlight, dreaming of spools of red hair tickling my nose and soft fair skin against my own. I dreamt I was sinking deeper and deeper in memory and lost in a small twin mattress of heaven with her, exchanging stares with her. I woke up with a sick feeling in my stomach that night. I stayed silent examining how sick I really was. I could stop hurting myself, but she hurt me. I picked at the wounds. I reclined my hair and recited the poem I wrote after we broke up:

> *"I left the record playing too long,*
> *Shell-shocked, alone I played our song.*
> *The entire house smells of burnt vinyl,*
> *To the soundtrack or your remembrance*
> *I held your recital"*

I glanced over at Tonka and distinctly remembered thinking how I could never share this with him. He'd never understand, I thought.

Somehow, along this trip, I blanked out. One second we were speeding through Chicago, the next we were in the burbs. We were going 25 mph through side-streets and foreign roads. My head pivoted from side to side like some idiot dodo bird. "Wha—" slipped out of my mouth like a fart from a small dog. "We're slowing down!" I narrated everything like a moron. We stopped on a street with a long, black metal fence. Tonka got out and stared into the distance. I sat in my seat like a five-year-old, seatbelt hugging me as if my mother buckled me in. Trying to get a better view of where we were, I moved my head in serpentine patterns. I saw a funeral. A woman wearing a black barrette connected eyes with Tonka from a hundred feet away. She looked to her ankles and then she turned away. Thirty more seconds of staring from Tonka and he got back into the car. We drove for about ten miles and we didn't say a word. I just stared at him like some sort of a stupid animal. I felt stupid and uninformed. On the tenth mile he said, "Her name is Diana." I closed my mouth for the first time in almost fifteen minutes. "I loved her," he went on. At this point I felt my bowels tie in knots then rattle around like a Yahtzee cup. After that, he just went on as if nothing ever happened. The previous events were the most natural thing in the world. Still, somehow, I felt like I should say something.

Within the first thirty miles across, the first sign we saw said, "Welcome to Iowa." Tonka stole me an ID from a man twenty-four years of age and looking absolutely identical to me. The expression on his face was like royalty, so I proudly flashed that ID to even police officers. There was no difference. It was six o'clock in the afternoon and it seemed like it would be daylight forever and it was the hottest the sun could provide without taking the baby hairs off. We stopped at a collaborated hipster-dive bar. I was eager to use my newfound treasure, the ID. Within seconds, I smelled a familiar smell of innocence and tulips penetrating my nasal passages into a fixation. I tried finding my way around the wasteland of leather jackets and fake eyelashes. It brought me to a section where every person had an aura of black rain clouds over their head like little circles of vultures. Faintly secluded in the corner was a heavy-like specter on a barstool. The spirit took on the physical appearance of a redheaded woman with long legs in a red sundress. My heart beat once, and then I hid in the corner. We

45

immediately connected eyes. She shared the same face as the girl who left me in dishonor. Pretending that I did not notice her, I found the nearest chair that faced away from her.

"Fate has a way with grabbing you by the wrist and throwing you, doesn't it?" The words came right from red lipstick to the back of my ear.

"I don't believe in fate," I said, speaking with accidental confidence that seemed to intrigue her.

Somehow, a man with confidence hijacked through my shoes and took over my body. We talked for a straight hour. I couldn't understand it. She looked just like her and she even smelled like her, but this one was wise. She was attracted to me and she smiled at me. However, it wasn't her. She looked so similar that it was as if I turned back the time. I could have her again.

It became my mission to kiss her that night. Her friend had knowledge of a party down the road, and we piled in our car. Tonka and I followed them to a barn from the dust bowl area in the farmlands. Around it were acres of dry dirt and dead grass. There were giant speakers, Chinese lanterns, and artsy Iowa youth dancing to Motown, Doo-wop, and old school hip-hop. She grabbed my wrist and pulled me into a dance. Within seconds of dancing, she kissed my lips, and then I died. Somehow, it felt like I was still living.

"By the way, my name is Veronica," she said in a humorous, ironic manner. I immediately heard cymbals strike in my imagination.

"And I'm waiting for a message from a girl by the name of Veronica," I quoted a Reckless Eric song in a corny British accent. I made an ass out of myself every time I tried to speak, but it made no difference. We both became microwave silly putty to one another.

That night, we left the party to watch the sun rise from a dried-out corn field. Tonka and Veronica's friend Emily were locked at the arm, smoking weed together. I was about a quarter mile away from the car with Veronica. We laid a blanket on the ground and kissed. With the breaths between, we looked into each other's eyes. When the sky turned dark blue and the stars were brighter than they had ever been, I fell asleep. I dreamt that time stood still. Just in happiness, I felt my worries about everything I left behind fade away like clarity on a foggy mirror.

DEUS EX MACHINA

Water doused my face like a tsunami. I scattered to my knees on the dirt ground, blinded by the merciless yellow son. It still felt like I was dreaming. Standing over me in prowess was Tonka. In his hands, he held a small metal bucket.

"What the f— is wrong with you?" I cursed at him.

"I want you to meet someone," he said still laughing. Looking tore up from the floor up, he looked pale as a ghost and was stammering his words.

Out from behind me, a glowing black silhouette circled into my line of vision. His long curly hair blocked out the sun. He smiled with a rolled cigarette in his mouth. He looked like a veteran from the Vietnam War but he was only thirty.

"Hey Pete. I'm Eli, Ton's cousin," he mumbled loudly. I remember thinking he sounded a lot like Shredder from Teenage Mutant Ninja Turtles. It was as if his voice was so raspy that it hurt him when he talked.

"What happened to California?" I blurted without formal introduction.

"F— California, man," Tonka replied. "I hate sitting in the car with your smelly ass for longer than I have to," he said jokingly.

"I thought I'd pack up and meet you guys halfway," Eli said, scratching his ear to his shoulder.

"Why would you drive so far out of your way?"

As I got up, I began to question everything about this strange circumstance.

"Why wouldn't you just meet us there?" I said looking at both of them.

Tonka gave me a scared look. All of a sudden, Eli finds us in the middle-of-nowhere-Iowa with no car and very few bags.

"I wanna know what the f— is going on." I demanded peace of mind.

As I scanned the makeshift campsite for more answers, I noticed that the girls were gone. Tonka looked like a stranger to me. His eyes were bloodshot and his face was bloated and pale with hinds of red and purple flush in his cheeks. I scanned Eli's forearms to find a garden of new and old track marks. I felt adrenaline rushing though my body like lightning.

"What's in the bag?" I said, biting my tongue. The next word I heard changed the course of my life.

"Don't worry about what's in the bag," he said as he put his hands behind his back. This was it. I was a young kid thrown into a sudden standoff with a mad man. Tonka fainted in the backseat and awoke as he hit the leather seat.

"It's drugs, Pete. I f—d up."

Apparently, this entire trip had been a drug run. Cases of Sudafed were in our trunk the entire time. In Eli's bag was a cinder block of heroin. Scattered amongst his person was enough coke to give us all felony charges. The Sudafed Tonka collected was to pay off Eli for everything he owed from abusing Eli's supply. I was the icing on the cake. I felt the blood rush through my arms like wild vines. I gripped my fist tight. I felt blood accumulate in the palm of my hands. To Eli, we were his foot soldiers. We were the drug dealers reporting to him. We were slaves of Tonka's debt. I studied Eli's physique and compared it to my own brawn. In my lifetime, thus far I only hit five people. I stared down Eli as he talked in threats and metaphors. Tonka lay in the back of the car weeping.

Wait, now this next moment changed the course of my existence. Truthfully, this is the moment I started to believe in, maybe, God or the universe pushing power to its human creation, but at this moment in time I created my own destiny.

Eli lit a cigarette out of the corner of his mouth. As I locked eyes with him, the moment was so quiet that I could hear his coarse mustache make noise against the cigarette. I moved my leg around to see if I still had the keys in my pocket. I did. Is everything in the car? Check. So much was going through my mind, but outside I could barely hear the wind. Somehow, judging by the way he kept putting his hands behind his back, I knew Eli had a gun tucked into the back of his pants. He felt so confident. To him, we were just a couple of kids with nowhere to go. However, I was ready. I felt my nails dig into my palms from gripping a fist so tightly. My knuckles were white when my moment came. Eli looked down as if I was given the green light. I charged at him like a bat out of hell, a demon Rottweiler, something unexplainable. I kicked up the dry dirt. I took him to the ground and dropped the sharpest part of my elbow to his chin in one continuous motion. As we both quickly got up his gun dropped near his feet, but he didn't notice. We were both covered in Eli's sweat and blood. As soon as he was back in my sight, I started running at him.

49

Simultaneously, he noticed his gun by stepping on it. He picked it up and before he could even point it at me, I drove my fist across his cheekbone so hard that when he hit the ground I figured him for dead. Tonka, still sick and looking like death, emptied our car of all illegal contraband, taking all the money from Eli's unconscious body and stashing it into the glove box. From there we were gone. Eli would never hear from me again.

JUSTIFIED MEANS

There I was, driving Tonka's car while he was puking in the back. I blocked out his moans, sped down the highway state-to-state and pedal-to-the-metal. Like a message from God, I felt my freed Indian-like spirit come back to me. Cherokee drum was beating again. Only this time it was faster and louder than ever. Every stop for gas was the only time we went to the bathroom. No more food. It was energy drinks the whole ride. I watched the sun go up, then down, then up again. After the first day, Tonka rose from his slumber. The DTs were hard, ask anybody. Bur when it's over you feel alive. He climbed up front and together we pushed the car to its limits. Every ten miles the car would make a different strange noise, but it kept going strong. Bartleby died that day, Deus ex Machina was reborn.

By the time we came back to Michigan, it was 5:45 a.m. Birds were everywhere. I saw life in a new way. At 6:30 a.m. I said goodbye to Tonka in front of his house. We hugged, shook hands, and then he walked to the front door giving me the peace sign and waving, not even turning the full way around.

"By the way, the car is stolen," he said as I started the car.

It was true, and that was the last time I ever saw Tonka again. At 7:00 a.m. I sat three blocks away from my house in

50

a stolen car. I took out all of my belongings and put the keys under the seat. After that, I surprised myself. What does one do after an adventure of bootleggers and guns? No sleep for days? He goes to school. I did. I went to school and I graduated.

As I finish typing these lines, I will be 22 years, 4 days, 10 hours, and 43 minutes old. Two weeks ago my cousin committed suicide. Two months ago, I drove a seventeen-year-old stranger to the emergency room because he was overdosing. Four months ago, I saved a baby from a car accident. These things are all true, but it's just another year, another year I am thankful for. The ending appears bleak, but as you can well imagine, the adventure continues. Never a dull moment. I will continue life collecting bit by bit the little white pieces of what.

Fin!

Bloody Summer

ZAHRAA AYOUB

People never forget painful memories that shredded their hearts. My tears flood every time I see or hear about war. A quick flash back takes me back to summer of 2006. I was born in Beirut, the capital of Lebanon, in 1995. I spent my summer vacations with my family in Maroon Al Rass, a small village in Southern Lebanon. However, summer 2006 was unusual. It was tragic, bloody, and scary.

In the summer of 2006, I was a ten-year-old girl. I didn't know that much about war, but that summer made me experience war. It all started on July 12, 2006, in Maroon Al Rass, on the border with Israel. I woke up to a regular morning, had breakfast, and sat with my grandmother. I found her glued to the chair in front of the TV, listening to the news. We watched together as a gruesome massacre took place in southern Lebanon, at the hands of Israel. The families that were killed had been seeking shelter from the bombing with the French forces that were part of the United Nations. However, the French refused to shelter them, leaving them prey to attack by the Israeli planes. About twenty people died that day; nine of them were children. I was terrified by the scene. There were children on the floor with no heads, missing limbs, and parents searching for their children. That sight made me wish I were blind. I had no idea why that was happening. It was the first time I had ever seen or heard anything like this. My grandmother started explaining everything to me about war and how both sides fight. She was only trying to prepare me for what might happen next. From what she said, it was then clear to me that war had started. I was scared of the bombing sounds so I started crying because I wanted my mother and my brothers. My uncle took me to my other grandparents' house, where my mother was. The streets were empty of people. We had to walk there because Israeli helicopters were bombing moving cars. Every step I took made me feel as if I were walking to my grave.

Two days later, we moved to my aunt's house because someone told my mom that the Israelis were going to bomb the huge building next to our house. Near my aunt's house, we met with United Nations soldiers. They were buying food as if they knew something was coming. My mom asked one of them if the war was going to last long, but she did not get a direct answer. The French soldier told my mom that they had no idea what was happening. A few hours later, Israeli helicopters bombed that building. The broken pieces of the building were scattered throughout the whole village. All who were in the market, which was few steps away from my aunt's house, ran down to the basement. Because we were scared, we fell over each other going down the stairs. My grandmother couldn't walk. We forgot her upstairs due to the shock. When we remembered her, three of us ran to get her because she was heavy. I sat in the corner scared. Everyone in the house was screaming and worried about their relatives. Although I tried to calm my brothers, the bombing was too loud to keep them calm. We all started praying for God to protect us.

Although the bombing was still going on, most people were running away to Sidon, about fifty miles away from the village. Some were going by car, others were walking. We stayed because driving was a great risk since Israel was bombing moving cars. Bombing intensified day after day. Deaths were rising, and food was becoming scarce. People told us that the house we were living in was likely to fall from any strong explosion. So we ran back to my grandfather's house. I was running with my head down, holding my mom's hand. There were about fifteen people in the same house. After nine days of the war, my cousin's house was burned while they were sleeping. A bomb had dropped from an Israeli plane into their living room. They had no place to go except our house, so our number increased to about twenty-three people. When the Israeli bombing subsided, kids played with each other and forgot what was happening outside. When the bombing intensified, we separated and each took a corner or we ran to our mothers with tearful eyes, hearts beating fast and bodies shaking.

The bombing increased to its maximum because Israel soldiers wanted to settle in our village. We heard much bombing that week, and each day the sound was getting more and more intense. Every time I asked my uncle where this bombing was, he told me that it was far and we were alright. But one day the glass in the second floor of the house broke. I was sure that the bombing was getting closer. The next morning we woke up to the sounds of screaming and shooting. We thought that the war was over and people were celebrating, but the truth was totally the opposite. The war had just started. Israeli soldiers were able to break into the village. They attacked my cousin's house and sprayed the whole house with bullets while my cousin's family was still in the house! Thank God that both families weren't injured. They were only terrified, and they ran to our home. At that moment the Israelis knew that there were people living in this house. More than two hundred Israeli soldiers surrounded the house. They started shooting the house from outside, and then my uncle heard the sound of a bomb inside the house. He told us not to panic. Few seconds later the bomb exploded and destroyed the whole bathroom. We started to move out of the house, holding a white banner and putting our hands up.

After everyone was out of the house, the soldiers started to shoot the house randomly and took out the doors and used them as shields. At the same time, they made us stand in a line next to each other. They took all the men, tied their hands, and started to interrogate them. They bombed the garage with the car inside it, but the car wasn't totally damaged. I was thinking that was going to be the last day in my life. They took us inside the house and separated women from men by putting men on the second floor and women on first floor in one room. When we first entered the house, it was chaotic. All the doors and windows were broken, the wall was full of bullet holes, and the furniture was scattered all over the place.

We had to stay living with the enemy for three days. It was the most humiliating thing that happened to us in our entire lives. Israeli soldiers accompanied us whenever we wanted to move from one room to another. For bathroom visits they waited in front of the door until we were done. We shared our water, food, and house with the people that were killing innocent people and making orphans of innocent children. Watching the Israeli soldiers shooting houses and people without mercy and not being able to stop them was very hard and painful.

As days were passing, our number increased until we became around forty people. Our big number forced us to divide the food between us in small amounts. In addition to that, sometimes we had to fast in order for the food to last longer. Moreover, we slept very close to each other because of the room's small size. Also we slept with all our clothes, even our shoes, so, in case something happened, we would be ready to run away.

One day, the water stopped running. So my brother, who is two years younger than I, went upstairs to get the water from the well. At the same time, Israeli soldiers fired a missile which frightened my brother so much that he almost fell in the well. My mom was four months pregnant when all of this started. She used to feel pain in her stomach, but she couldn't do anything about it. The day the Israeli soldiers entered our house, she started seeing blood, and she had no medicine nor was there a hospital to help her. The next morning she found herself all covered in blood. She said that when she went to the bathroom, the bleeding increased to the extent that she was passing big clumps of blood. My mother thought that she had lost her baby and felt that no baby could have survived all the stress and pain she had gone through.

A couple of days later, we woke up to complete silence. We went out of the room and did not find any soldiers; they were all gone. So we went upstairs and freed the men who were trapped on the second floor. My mother's uncle told us that we had to leave the house as fast as possible because the house might be booby-trapped.

We sent a little boy to see if my uncle and his family were still in their house. My grandmother stood on a small hill to keep her eyes on the boy. On his way back home, my grandmother waved to him so he would come back. When Israeli soldiers saw her they thought that she was giving a signal to someone, so they shot her in her back. She crept to the front of the house until my uncle's wife who saw her started to shout and scream. Everybody came out to see the reason for the screaming, except for the children who were kept inside in order that they not panic. My relatives found my grandmother on the floor covered with blood. We had to do something in order to save her life. First, we covered the wound with a piece of cloth to stop the bleeding. Then, we covered her with a blanket because she felt cold. She wanted water, but we couldn't give it to her, since it could increase her bleeding. Suddenly we heard the soldiers telling us that we had three minutes to leave the house. We were completely shocked. What should we do? How could we take my grandmother while she was injured? Were they going to kill us all? All these questions passed through our minds, but we couldn't continue to panic. My mom started shouting to the soldiers that we had an injured person and we needed an ambulance. They responded by telling us that we had only have two minutes to leave or they would bring the house down on our heads. We had no choice but to obey their orders.

We continued to walk towards my uncle's house. With each step we took, we were filled with anxiety about what might be awaiting us. Once there, the soldiers separated the men from the women again. It took a lot of time, and every time we tried to tell them about my grandmother they would silence us and not let us talk. But eventually they listened to us.

"We have a wounded person," my mom said furiously.

"Where is she?" one of them asked.

"We left her in the other house because we did not want to move her. It would have hurt her," my mom answered.

"Who shot her?" the other soldier asked my mom sarcastically.

"I do not know. Why don't you ask them yourself?" my mom answered him.

"Two of you go get her and come back," they said after long discussions.

They went and got her, but there was no way to get her down except by placing her on a hard surface. They found a door lying on the floor and used it to move her.

"Do you have a car?" the soldier asked my uncle.

"Yes I have," my uncle said, puzzled.

"Go to the edge of the village next to the border, and they will help you there."

My uncle drove his car and took my grandmother, but they did not allow him to cross the border. So he went back and told the soldiers what had happened. They told him that he had gone to the wrong place. He went back, but this time to the right place. Before he reached the border he stopped the car and, carrying my grandmother, walked toward the border. Her blood covered his hands, and he had no idea what he was doing. All he wanted was for his mom to get better. Suddenly, he heard voices shouting, "Are you crazy? Come back!" They were the United Nations soldiers. He did not care and continued on his way until he reached the border. The officials at the border allowed him to pass because they knew he was coming. They took my grandmother in the ambulance to Israel and treated her. We had no idea what happened to them or whether she was alive or not. All what we knew was that we had to stay in a house next to the Israeli soldiers.

The first day passed normally. We all adjusted to the house and had some rest, but we weren't able to forget what had happened to my grandmother. The next day was troubling; there was no food and no water. All that we could find was some cheese and dried figs. Since we were not allowed to go out of the house, we needed some way to tell the Israeli soldiers that we were out of food and water. So we wrote on a tissue with lipstick that we wanted water; but they didn't respond to us even though they saw what we wrote, since they were watching us all the time. Even though my mother was pregnant, she was brave enough to disobey the soldiers and went the next morning holding a hose that she had to put into a well to suck the water, until it ran freely.

During that same day, we increased in number by about eight people. People from our village also suffered as we had and even worse. When they reached our house they were horrified and full of fear. The soldiers told them to go to the house we were in and then they would then tell us what to do. When the people arrived, they told us the whole story, but instead of feeling relieved that they were alive, our fear only became more intense. We were just waiting and wondering what the Israelis were going to do to us and whether we would survive or not. Our numbers increased and still there was no food supply to feed us all, so the women decided to make bread with the plain flour they found. It was the only source of food for us at that moment. A few days later, everything was silent. We found out that the soldiers had left the house next to us, so my mom told our cousin to go to check to see if there was food where the soldiers had been living. All he found was a ransacked house; all the windows were broken, and the doors, too, were used as protection from bombs. The most disgusting things he found were cans and bottles full of urine and feces. Thankfully he found cans of food that we could use, and there were enough to feed us.

The most painful days I have ever lived were at that house; everyone used to have nightmares, and some days we couldn't sleep because of the intensity of the bombing. I once woke up to the sound of tanks passing beside the house, and I immediately closed my eyes so I wouldn't feel the pain if the house collapsed on us. I could hear every bomb that was dropped, even in the neighboring villages. I always felt the intensity of the bombing by the gust of air that would enter from under the door. But we all had to stay strong and stand by one another.

Using a radio that ran on batteries was the only way we had to know what was going on. The radio announced that there was a truce for forty-eight hours. Everyone knew that staying after the announcement was suicide, so we decided to leave. Some of us said it was better to go to the United Nations in our village, and others wanted to go to the village adjacent to us. My family and about fifteen others decided to go to the United Nations office because there was no transportation and my mom was pregnant. We children were small, so we could never walk the twenty miles to the United Nations Center. My mom was afraid that we wouldn't find anyone in the center; the area was abandoned due to its being close to the border. The streets were all destroyed; there was no sign of a road, nothing but sand and left over pieces of burned tanks and missiles. When we reached the United Nations Center, we stood outside waiting for someone to notice us. The gate was huge and high so no one could enter. We spent hours shouting that we needed help, that we had sick children and they needed food and diapers. They finally were given orders to open the door for us because we told them that we were American passport holders. My mom showed them her driver's license so they would actually believe us. The United Nations soldiers were very polite and helpful; they fed us and allowed us to take baths after weeks with no bath, so we actually felt a little relaxed and forgot that we were living in a war. We children spent the whole time playing and having fun. After four days of staying there, we had to move because the United Nations Center's resources were exhausted. They moved us by tank to another center that was in a village called Tebnine, twenty-eight minutes from my village. One of the soldiers there was a doctor, so my mom asked him to examine her so she could check on the baby. He told her that there was no heartbeat, but she should get checked by a hospital because he didn't have the right instruments. My dad wasn't with us; he was in the United States because he used to work there. When he saw on the news that my grandmother had been injured, he got worried and afraid that something could have happened to us. He wasn't able to call us or get exact information about our condition, but rumors had spread about us. Some people told him that they saw the house we were living in completely destroyed, others told him that we were in a village far away. He was shocked and completely devastated, but he didn't lose hope in finding us alive. When we were in Tebnine, we were able to contact him and comfort him that we were alright. He was very relieved to hear our voices, but was still worried because the war wasn't over and we were still in danger.

Two days later, the United Nations soldiers took us, by tank, to Sidon because it was safer there. On the way, we realized that our green south has turned into a black, gloomy place; all the fields, homes, shops were burned and turned to ashes.

However, in Sidon there had not been such intense bombing, so the soldiers left us in Sidon, and from there we could find a place to stay. There were a huge number of people, all of them seeking a place to keep them safe and alive. While we were waiting for them to find us a place, we found that our uncle and grandmother were also there. It was a great relief to see them, and to know that they were not harmed. In the meantime, my grandfather eventually found us a place to spend the night; it was an incomplete house which had no doors and no windows, but it was better than nothing. After that, my grandfather found an old house and rented it from its owners so we could settle down. We stayed in Sidon for about ten days, living a normal life, as if there were no war. The people were so nice there; they welcomed us with open hearts and with love. They let us take showers in their homes, made us food, and loaned us some clothes.

On one of these days, we went to the shops to get some clothes other than the ones we were wearing. While we were there, my cousin, who was five years old, got lost, and we spent the whole day searching for him. We checked in the hospitals, the delicatessen, streets, shops, playgrounds, and everywhere he could have gone. My uncle was really terrified that he might not find him. Finally, we found him in the city offices, where the woman who had found him had taken him. We couldn't handle any more shocks; everything we had lived through was too much to handle.

Later on, my dad's brothers were able to call us and check if we were alright. They advised us to come to the place where they were living, which was much safer, and from there we would be able to travel to America, in case the war lasted long. But going to my uncles' was a great risk. The war hadn't ended, and the roads were not safe. Luckily, they announced a truce, and it was safer for us to leave, although it was very difficult for us to leave our grandparents. We said our goodbyes with eyes full of tears, but there was nothing else we could do. Finding a cab to take us to our uncles' place was a problem. No one was willing to take that risk. But, eventually, a good man was willing to take us, and of course we paid him, too. Our uncles were very relieved when they saw us; they wouldn't travel with their families to the United States until they found us and knew we were alright. The war was coming to its end and we were still with our uncles.

Israel finally announced that it was going to leave Lebanon after one day, but that day was a nightmare to all Lebanese people. They bombed our villages, streets, and buildings so hard and intensely that the sky turned black from the smoke and fumes. That one day was more intense than all the days of the war combined. Some people thought there was no way

63

Israel was going to bomb that much, so they returned to their original houses and then wished they hadn't gone back. Many people were killed that day; it was a complete catastrophe.

Even though the war was over, we didn't know if we should feel happy or feel sad. People had died or lost limbs, or faced life with deformity. Houses were destroyed, and streets were wrecked. We went back to our house in Beirut, and I was so happy it was in one piece. But looking around at all the destruction stole my happiness away. All green and shiny, Beirut had become a ghost house, all gloomy and horrifying. No words could have explained how we Lebanese people felt, the amount of pain we were in, and the agony of our loss. No pain is comparable to that of a mom who lost her son, a girl or boy losing their parents, a friend losing her/his best friend. We were lucky no one I knew died or got injured, but others had lost their complete families.

The 2006 war lasted thirty-four days and was a nightmare. I was glad that it was over and no one in my family was hurt. That war made me wish for the impossible. I wished to be a one-year-old child so none of these painful memories would remain. The war of 2006 was barbaric. It not only affected generations that lived it, but it is going to affect the new generation. Thirteen hundred people were killed, and a huge number of people were injured, and nature and the environment were destroyed. That is why the summer of 2006 was a bloody summer.

Day by day, life returned to normal. Lebanese people were determined to make their country bloom again, and better than ever. They all stood hand-to-hand to build their houses, fix their streets, and forget what had happened to them. This all required time and patience, but the Lebanese were willing to dust off the misery of war and stand stronger than ever. They were not ready to allow Israel to be proud of what they had done to them but, instead, they made them regret the day they decided to have a war. It was a great victory for the Lebanese; regardless of all the things that happened, we stood strong and didn't let go of our country.

The World Is Not Enough

Jarrett Henderson

Growing up in a dysfunctional household in Detroit, Michigan was not easy at all for me. Both of my parents were abusive drug addicts. My sister was always running the streets, chasing behind boys. My brother was part of the street life. I was the youngest of the family and I saw a lot since the early years of my life. My father, Lamont, had left us, and so did my sister, Rocky, and my brother, Mario. Only my mother, Larine, and I stayed together. She didn't know how to handle that, and neither did I. Because drugs became a big part of her life, school was not a priority for me. I wanted to do the right thing with my life but I let the streets influence me to make the wrong decisions. I started selling drugs. I robbed goods from people. I also broke into homes.

Growing up in these mean streets of Detroit, Michigan was not easy for me. Hell, it wasn't easy for no one. Either you were in the streets doing the wrong thing or you were in the house studying and doing homework. I chose to do the wrong thing with my life. I had my Auntie Sharon who was trying to help me get my life in order, but by then I was so far gone. I wasn't ready to listen to anyone. I moved from house to house trying to find that inner peace, but it was hard to find. I never had that feeling of a place that I could call home. As I got older, I thought I was doing pretty good for myself but really I was setting myself up for failure.

In the year 2000, I was charged with the attempt to distribute five hundred grams of marijuana. Because it was my first time ever being in trouble, the judge gave me two years' probation. I also had to attend meetings that would help me overcome my problems. That only lasted for a short period of time because the street life was calling me. I jumped back into the streets fast. All types of things were going on in my life, but I didn't give a care. I just was looking at the money that I was making. Now that I look back on my life, that money was nothing. I found myself back in trouble a year later. This time I was being charged by the U.S. government. I was indicted for drug trafficking. I didn't realize how much trouble I was in until I saw two white gentlemen, Officer Wright and Officer Jones, come in and read me my rights. I was found guilty on two counts and I was sentenced to 13 and a half years in a federal prison. At that time I felt like my life was over with. I thought I would never see the streets of Detroit again. I didn't know what this journey was going to be like.

Going through that experience taught me a lot. I got involved with some good people when I was incarcerated. I met men by the name of C-X and T-X. C-X and T-X were part of the Nation of Islam. These brothers of mine helped show me what being a man is all about and what God was expecting from me once I was released. Before I was incarcerated, I never tried to hear this kind of talk, but I was forced to hear this knowledge because I believe this is what God had planned for me. I started studying the Bible and the Quran with these brothers, but I never became a part of any religion. I just listened to the message that I was receiving and studying and I was applying it to my life. I found myself finding peace in prison. I was able to think better. I could smell the fresh air when I went outside, and I could hear better when people talked to me.

There were some hard times while I was incarcerated. I had lost my brother Mario and my nephew Tone-Tone to the street life. I asked God to keep my family strong through those tough times. That was one of the hardest things about being in prison. I just never knew if my loved ones were going to make it out there while I was in there. However, I was blessed to have both of my parents staying alive and waiting for me with open arms. April the third I was released from prison. The sun was shining down on me really hard. I saw my mother first, then I saw my father. I cried like a baby. It was tears of joy that I was feeling. My mother and father were crying. When I got home, I smelled some good old soul food in the kitchen being prepared for me. My sister and my aunties were in the kitchen cooking some fried chicken, macaroni and cheese, collard greens, and some cornbread. We sat around, talked, and laughed all night.

The next morning it was time for business. I went out applying for jobs everywhere. It was really hard for me my first few months home because I could not find a job anywhere. Before I was released from prison, one of my mentors explained how hard it would be to find a job. He reminded me to keep my faith in God. When I came home, I went back to my old neighborhood. Everything was looking bad. It looked like a hurricane had come through and tore every house apart. The people I used to hang out with were either dead, in prison, on drugs, or doing the same thing as when I left. It was a sad thing to see but it was a reality check for me. I knew that I could no longer go back to that lifestyle. After a couple of months went by I found my first job at Two Men and a Truck and I was very happy. I thanked God for this blessing. Soon after that, I found my first love who is now my wife, my best friend, and my everything. She helped me with many things. I could never thank God enough for this woman. So here I am, three years later. I have God in my life, I have a beautiful wife, my own house, a car, and I have a job, plus I'm in college. Here is a rerun of my life story. Be prepared for all kinds of reactions to my story, but no matter what you feel, I hope you will be inspired to do the right thing and lift someone out of the ashes.

At Larina's home on Roselawn, Larina and I were sitting at the kitchen table talking about responsibility.

    Larine: [impatiently] Jarrett, I don't want you hanging out all night. What time will you be back home?

    Jarrett: [irritated] I don't know, Mother. We don't have school none this week. I'm going over Turk's house to hang out with him for a while.

    Larine: [wearily] Well you make sure you're not out there all night. I worry about you son.

    Jarrett: [tightly] I'll be fine, Mama. You just get some rest.

    Larine: You heard what I said, boy.

    Jarrett: Okay, what time will dad be home, Mama?

    Larine: Why?

    Jarrett: I just wanted to know. I'll see you later.

    Larine: Okay.

    Jarrett: [angrily to himself] I'm not coming home tonight. Hell, all my parents do is fight anyway. I don't have time for that!

Jarrett leaves and goes walking to his friend's house on Joy Road. When Jarrett arrives, Turk is sitting on the porch.

    Jarrett: Turk, wazup boy?

    Turk: Wazup playboy?

    Jarrett: [teasing] I can't call it. You ready to get this money?

Turk: The question is, is you ready to get this money?

Jarrett: I was born ready.

Turk: What time you got to be back home?

Jarrett: [in a serious tone of voice] I'm not going home tonight. I'm kicking it with you tonight.

Turk: [tightly] Okay, but you know how your mama is! I can't have her coming around here acting all crazy and shit.

Turk was older then Jarrett was by a few years. He had his own house at the age of 20, and Jarrett was 17. He knew Jarrett was a hustler. That's why he didn't care if he stayed at his house some nights.

Jarrett: Call Bub up and see wazup with that fool.

Turk: [defensively] You call that fool up yourself.

Jarrett: Why you don't like Bub?

Turk: 'Cause it's something about that boy. I'm trying to tell you.

Jarrett: Bub is cool, bro. That boy is getting money for real.

Turk: So? I am too.

Jarrett: Whatever bro.

Jarrett: [speaking on the phone] Bub, wazup boy? Come through. We on the block.

Bub: Give me like an hour and I'll be through there.

Jarrett: Bet.

Turk: [upset] One day you will listen to me, little homie.

Jarrett: I always do.

Bub invites Jarrett and Turk to a party.

Bub: What's up, fools? What's up for tonight? My girl is having a party tonight. Y'all should come through.

71

Jarrett: You know I'll be there.

Turk: I'm good, bro. I'm gonna get this money all night.

Jarrett: I knew that fool wasn't going to go, but it's all good. I'll be there for sure, Bub.

Bub: Bet. I'll see y'all boys later. I'm about to go to the mall and get fresh on y'all fools.

Bub leaves and Jarrett stays with Turk.

Jarrett: That was just like Bub. He always trying to outdo everybody when come to dressing up.

Turk: The block is banging today. Everybody must have gotten their checks today.

Jarrett: I know, right? Hell, I have made $600 already and I only been out here three hours. This is what 'am talking about.

Turk: So, you going to that party tonight with your boy Bub, huh?

Jarrett: You know it. You should stop acting like a lame and roll with us, fool. You know what to do.

Turk: Maybe next time, shorty. You be safe out here tonight. You know how them fools can get.

Jarrett: You know it. I keep my 9 mm on me at all times.

As Jarrett is discussing where he is going for the night, Rocky talks to her Mom.

Rocky: Mama, why can't I never go out with my friends? You let Jarrett and Mario always hang out with their friends!

Larine: [firmly] Last time I checked I was the mother and you was the daughter. I don't have to answers that question.

Mario: [upset at being mentioned] Keep my name out of your mouth, girl.

Rocky: [in an angry tone of voice] Shut up, Mario. Y'all get on my nerves around here.

Mario: Mama, I'll be back in a little while.

Larine: If you see your bother out there, tell him not to forget about what I said, OK?

Mario: Okay. Goodbye, Rocky. Love you.

As Mario leaves, Rocky keeps complaining about how it is not fair that she cannot go out with her friends.

Rocky: You see what I mean, Mama? This is not fair at all, and I'm telling Daddy when he get home from work.

Larine: On who? Don't make me come in there, girl.

As Larine speaks to Rocky about her smart mouth, Mario yells out for his mother.

Mario: Mama, Mama! The police just arrested Jarrett.

Larine: Oh no, what happen Mario?

Mario: I don't know, Mama. They say he got caught up in raid over there at Turk's house selling drugs.

Larine: Y'all father is going to kill me. Which jail is he at, boy?

Mario: I don't know, Mama. Maybe the one around the corner.

Mario leaves. Larine hurries to the police station. Looking angry and worried, she speaks to the officer.

Larine [loudly and angrily]: I'm going to kill this boy. Excuse me, officer, I was wondering if you had my son Jarrett Henderson in custody?

Officer: What's your son's name, Ms.?

Larine: Jarrett Henderson.

Officer: Yes. He's being charged with the attempt to distribute five hundred grams of marijuana, and we can't release him until he sees a judge in the morning.

Larine: What? What do you mean you can't release him? You have my son back there, sir, and I want him home with me now!

Officer: I'm sorry Ms., but I can't help you. He has to see a judge first.

Larine: Okay. What time will that be, officer?

Officer: 9:00 a.m., Ms.

Larine: Thanks, officer.

Officer: You're welcome, Ms.

The father comes and sees Rocky standing alone in front of the house.

Lamont: Where is your mother and brothers at, Rocky?

Rocky: Jarrett got arrested tonight, and they went to go see about him, and I don't know where Mario is at, Daddy. Daddy, why can't I go out and hang with my friends?

Lamont: What do you mean your brother got arrested? For what? And I don't want to hear nothing about you and your friends right now.

Rocky: I don't know what's going on, Daddy. Mario came and told us about what happen.

Lamont: This is what I be talking about. I have to come home to this shit every night. It's always something. I'm tired of this shit!

As he was speaking to Rocky, Larine arrives.

74

Lamont: Where is my son at, Larine?

Larine: Your son is right where he should be: in jail. Since he wants to be a drug dealer, he has to see the judge in the morning.

Lamont: I told you about letting these boys hang out in them streets anyway, and where the hell is Mario's ass at?

Larine: How the hell am I suppose to know? I can't keep up these damn boys no more.

Lamont: I can't take this shit no more. I don't think we're going to make it anymore, Larine.

Larine: So you're just going to leave your family?

Lamont: I have to for now. I need to get my life together. It's not the kids I'm leaving; it's you. I'm sorry, but I have to get myself together.

Larine: Fine, get the hell out of my house right now!

Mario comes in and he sees and hears his parents quarreling.

Mario: What's going on, Dad?

Lamont: I have to go, son. Me and your mother are giving each other a break.

Rocky: Please, Daddy, don't go!

Larine: Let him go, girl. We don't need him here with us.

Mario: I'm leaving too then. I can't take this shit anymore.

Larine: You know what? All y'all get the hell out my house right now!

Rocky: What about me, Mama?

Larine: You too! I take care of Jarrett by my damn self!

In his jail cell, Jarrett is talking to himself.

Jarrett: I wonder what my parents are thinking. I know my father is going to kill me. I can't wait to see this judge this morning.

The police bring Jarrett into the courtroom.

Judge: Since this is your first offense, Mr. Henderson, I'm going to sentence you to two years' probation.

Jarrett: [murmuring] Hell yeah! Let me out of here right now!

Larine and Jarrett arrive at the house.

Larine: [angrily] I want you to go right in your room, and don't come out until I tell you to!

Jarrett: Yeah, Mama. Where is everybody at, Mama?

Larine: Your father left us and so did your brother and sister. We don't need them. Now go to your room.

Jarrett: Damn, everybody left us just like that? I was only gone for a day.

Lamont: I want to see my son, Larine.

Larine: He's back there in his room.

Lamont: Hey, I want you to understand something, son. I have to go away. Me and your mother is not going to make it as a family. I need to get my life together, so I don't want you to think that I'm leaving you, because I'm not. Once I get everything together I want you to come live with me, okay? But in the mean time I need for you to stay out of trouble. I don't want you to go down the same road as your brother, okay?

Jarrett wanted to cry, but couldn't find the words.

Jarrett: Okay?

Lamont: I'll see you this week end, okay?

Jarrett: Okay? Love you, Dad.

Lamont: Love you more, son!

Larine: Okay, visiting hours are over with Lamont. Get the hell out of my house!

Jarrett was hurt. Who was going to help his mother and him out around here now?

Jarrett: I got to get this money now for real!

Larine: Come eat, boy. We have to talk! Now I want you to hear me and hear me good. I don't want you hanging out in them streets anymore. I'll find a way for us to make it. Do you hear me?

Jarrett: Yes, Mama. Is Rocky and Mario coming back home?

Larine: No, your sister wants to chase behind boys, and your brother wants to sell drugs, and I just can't take it anymore!

Jarrett listens to her, but his mind is on the streets. He wants to make something happen and happen fast.

Larine: Do you hear me, boy?

Jarrett: Yes, Mama.

Larine: Okay. Now I want to go get ready for school in the morning.

Jarrett: Okay.

Jarrett goes to see Turk at the latter's house.

Jarrett: What's up, Turk?

Turk: What's up, playboy? I see you made it out!

77

Jarrett: You know it.

Turk: So what happen?

Jarrett: They gave me a two years' probation.

Turk: That's what's up. Now what's up with you?

Jarrett: I need to get this money, bro. I can't do school no more. My father, sister, and brother left me and my mother. Now it's just us.

Turk: Damn.

Jarrett: I know, but it's all good. I'm gonna hold it down now!

Turk: I got you, bro. If you need anything, just let me know. Okay?

Jarrett: I'm glad you said that. What's up with that driving job?

Turk: You tryin' to get money for real now?

Jarrett: I got to, bro.

Turk: Okay. Give me a few days. I got something going down this weekend.

Jarrett: Okay, but in the meantime I got to get me some money now.

Turk: Let's get it then.

Jarrett: [thinking to himself] It is time to for me to go back home. I really don't feel like doing this, but I have to because I don't want to hear my mother's mouth. [to Turk]: I'm out, Turk.

Turk: Okay, I'll see you in the morning.

Jarrett: Alright.

Jarrett goes home. His mother is in her room but he does not see her.

Jarrett: [loudly] Mama, I'm home. Where is this lady at? [He goes to the table and sees drugs in a plastic bag]

Look at this shit. I knew she was using drugs, but I never seen it in the house before. I should leave too. I see enough of this shit on the streets and now I come home to this shit. It's on now.

Larine: What is you doing home?

Jarrett: I live here! What is this stuff, Mama?

Larine: Boy, don't worry about it. Go to your room!

Jarrett: [to himself] I can't wait to hit this road this weekend with Turk.

The next day Larine sits with him at the kitchen table. She opens an envelope.

Larine: What the hell? I can't believe this shit!

Jarrett: What's wrong, Mama?

Larine: We're being evicted. I asked your father to take care of this until I got on my feet. I guess he said the hell with us!

Jarrett: Damn. I got to make something happen fast!

Jarrett: [speaking to his dad on the phone] Daddy, what happen with you paying the rent for us? We're being evicted.

Lamont: I didn't have the money. You're going to go live with your Auntie Sharon for a while.

Jarrett: But what about Mama?

Lamont: She's going to go live with her friend Ms. Lady.

Jarrett: [to himself] Damn. It's always something. I still got to get this money.

Jarrett goes to Turk.

Turk: What's up, bro?

Jarrett: We're getting evicted soon. We still on for this weekend?

Turk: You know it. You ready?

Jarrett: Hell yeah. I'm ready! I got to go live with my Auntie over here on Joy Road and Southfield, but I'll be back over here to get this money with you.

Turk: Alright, that's what's up.

Jarrett: Well, I'm out. I'll see you this weekend, bro.

Turk: You know it.

Jarrett goes back home. His father arrives minutes after him and calls on him from the door.

Lamont: You ready, son?

Jarrett: Yeah, I'm ready.

Larine: Don't worry, baby. Mama is going to work everything out for us. You be a good boy now. I don't want you getting into any trouble now, you hear me?

Jarrett: Yes, Mama. I hear you. I love you Mama!

Larine: I love you more, baby!

Jarrett goes with his dad to Auntie Sharon's home.

Auntie Sharon: Hey Jarrett.

Jarrett: Hey, Auntie Sharon.

Auntie Sharon: Tomorrow I'm going to take you to your new school.

Jarrett: I don't want to change schools.

Auntie: You have to. The other school is too far for you.

Jarrett: [to himself] Damn. How is this going to work out now? How am I going to get this money if I'm not in the hood anymore? I'm just going to have to find a way because I'm not about to stop getting this money for nobody! This is all I can say.

The next day Jarrett starts going to Cody High School. This school has some beautiful girls that go here. Too bad he isn't going to be here long. Jarrett sees this one girl. She is beautiful. He goes up to her.

Jarrett: Excuse me, sweetie, but you are beautiful as hell! What is your name?

Girl: My name is Audria. And yours?

Jarrett: Jarrett.

Audria: Nice to meet you, Jarrett. I never seen you around here before. Is this your first day?

Jarrett: Yes it is. Do you have a boyfriend?

Audria: No I don't. Do you have a girlfriend?

Jarrett: [with a smile] I do now.

Andria: What you mean, "you do now?"

Jarrett: I would like for you to be my girlfriend.

Audria: Boy, you don't even know me.

Jarrett: Well, can I get to know you then?

Audria: You can call me later.

Jarrett: Okay, I'll do that. Wait a minute, you mean to tell me it's two of y'all?

Audria: That's my twin sister Adria.

Jarrett: [to himself]: That's what's up. Twin sisters!

Jarrett: Okay, I'll call you later, sweetie.

Audria: Okay.

Jarrett: [to himself] This school thing might not be too bad after all.

In his Auntie's home after school.

Auntie Sharon: How was school?

Jarrett: It was good. I met this girl today, Auntie, and she was beautiful.

Auntie Sharon: That's good.

The next morning Jarrett does not go to school. He goes to the hood with Turk to get this money. Jarrett doesn't go to school for the rest of that week. It is time for him to take this road trip with Turk. He is going to have to lie to his Auntie and tell her something every day when he is home after school time.

Auntie Sharon: How was school today?

Jarrett: It was good. Auntie, is okay if I go over and stay at friend house this weekend?

Auntie Sharon: I don't know about that. Let me think about it. Who is this friend you're talking about?

Jarrett: His name is Turkey.

Auntie Sharon: You can go, but I'm going to need his parents' number, okay?

Jarrett: Okay.

Jarrett goes to Turk's house and tells him that his Aunt Sharon is going to call.

Jarrett: We got to find a lady that has to act like your mother when my Auntie call your house.

Turk: That's nothing, bro. I got somebody for that. She going to ride with us to Ohio.

Jarrett: Okay.

Turk: Now you getting money, boy. It's time to go to the mall and get you fresh for school.

Jarrett: I see you got jokes, but it's cool. Let's go.

Jarrett starts going on the road with Turk a lot. They are getting a lot of money. Jarrett needs somewhere to put his money. He finds a place in his Auntie's backyard that works out good for him.

The day he goes to school, he is well dressed. He sees Audria in the hallway, but she doesn't want to talk to him. He goes to her.

Jarrett: What's wrong, girlfriend?

Audria: I haven't heard from you in two weeks.

Jarrett: [lying] My mother wasn't feeling good, and I had to go take care of her.

Audria: You could have called me.

Jarrett: You're right, sweetie. From now on, I'll make sure I call you every day. [Jarrett could tell she liked him and he liked her too.] You have the prettiest skin that I have ever seen. Can I take you and your sister out to lunch today?

They go out to lunch and have a good time. The next morning Jarrett walks over to her house to walk to school with her and her sister. He does that every day. They get serious about each other, but Jarrett is still in the streets. She was not like the rest of the girls Jarrett befriended.

When he leaves Audria, he receives a call from his mom.

Larine: Hey, baby. How you been? I haven't heard from you in a few weeks, son. Everything okay with you over there?

Jarrett: Yes, Mama. Just been going to school every day.

Larine: That's good, son. I miss you.

Jarrett: I miss you too, Mama. Have you heard from Rocky and Mario?

Larine: I seen them the other day, and they asked about you.

83

Jarrett: They did? When you see them again tell them to
    call me please?
Larine: I will. You just make sure that you're being good. I
    love you son.
Jarrett: Okay, Mama. I love you too. Bye.

Jarrett receives another call. It is Turk who is on the line this time.

Turk: You ready for this weekend? This one is going to be
    big, bro.
Jarrett: I'm always ready to get this money, bro.
Turk: Okay, I'll be to get you around 7:00 a.m.
Jarrett: Okay.

*Jarrett is on his way back from Ohio when he gets pulled over by
the state police. He does not know what to do. He does not know
if he should run or not. He has 50 pounds of marijuana in the car
he is driving. He pulls over.*

Officer: Step out of the car, sir.
Jarrett: [with a straight face] Is everything okay, Officer?
Officer: [from a distance] Step out of the car, sir.

One of the officers searches the car and finds the marijuana.

Officer: You are under arrest for possession of drugs.

*The officers take Jarrett to jail. He did not think it was that bad.
"It's only marijuana," he thinks. They call his Auntie and tell her
what is going on. They tell her that Jarrett should be in Detroit in
the morning at the Federal Courthouse.*

Auntie Sharon: Lamont, your son was in Ohio driving with some drugs. The officer said that he would be at the Federal Courthouse in the morning. I can't do this shit, Lamont.

Lamont: Damn. Okay, I'll call his mother and let her know what's going on.

Lamont: [speaking to Larine on the phone] Larine, your son is back in trouble again. This time it's federal, and we have to go to the Federal Court House in the morning.

Larine: What? I can't do this shit again. He told me he was doing well over there and going to school, Lamont.

In jail, Jarrett knew what Turk was thinking. He was thinking that Jarrett was going to tell on him, but Jarrett wanted to be true to this game! Jarrett was also thinking about his baby, Audria. He knew she would not want to talk to him anymore after hearing what happened to him. On top of that, his parents were going to go crazy on him. What was going to happen with his family and his girl worried him a lot.

Jarrett appears in court the following day. His parents and Audria are there. The judge read Jarrett's case and tells him that he is going to send him to prison this time.

Jarrett: [whispering to his lawyer] How much time are we looking at?

Lawyer: [whispering] Because you were in another state, you could get up to 20 years in prison.

Jarrett: [looking at his lawyer like he is crazy] I didn't kill no damned body, man!

When the judge announced the sentence, he gave Jarrett thirteen and a half years in prison. Jarrett cried like a baby. Everybody came to see him. Even Audria came to see him. They talked, and she explained that she could not wait for him that long. He understood, but he did tell her that he loved her and that he was coming to her when he comes home from prison. She cried hard, and he started to cry when he was taken to serve his time in prison.

Things Look Different from My Perspective

Khodr Farhat

BORN DIFFERENT

Do you know the difference between day and night? Do you know the difference between dark and light? I don't. I have spent twenty years of my life looking for hope without losing hope. My name is Khodr Farhat. I was born In Beirut, Lebanon on June 8, 1993 and I have been legally blind since birth! My parents were expecting that because I have two sisters that are visually impaired too. Majida is the older sibling. She graduated from the Arab University of Beirut with a Law degree. Yassmine came second. At first, she majored in English Literature and Linguistics at Open Arab University in Beirut. She changed her mind and she is now majoring in Special Education. She attends Henry Ford College with me.

FAMILY SUPPORT IN THE ARABIC CULTURE

My dad, Majid, is a great role model for me. He spent most of his life working for the sake of keeping us satisfied and happy! He encountered many dangerous situations, especially during the Lebanese Civil War back in the 1970s and 1980s. I have heard all the incidents that happened to him on his way to and from work at the Beirut International Airport. One day, for example, he was driving on the highway, and the snipers were everywhere! They shot anyone and anything they saw moving on the street. Even cats and dogs were targets. They had no mercy. He escaped several times. He did not have any choice. He had plenty of responsibilities on his shoulders. I always pray to keep him safe because he is a great man! No one who asked him for help was ever turned down. My mom, Fatme, is a very sacrificing woman. She is very strong. Dealing with three disabled children as well as other duties is not easy at all. She is a real mother. I ask God to extend her life because she deserves the best from us.

My family is very supportive. I got all the help I needed when I was little. My dad took me to the best well-known doctors in Lebanon. He provided everything for me. My mom was there for me all the time, too; whether I was happy or sad, healthy or sick, troubled or peaceful, she was my source of strength. Majida has vision problems, but she is still able to read print. She used to help me with any visual matter. Yassmine reads Braille, so she helped me along the way in school until I reached fourth grade, when I started to depend on myself.

NO ACCOMMODATIONS IN A POOR COUNTRY

I still have some bitter memories regarding school. I remember everything from that time. I was not eligible to register in any public school in Lebanon due to my disability. I had to attend private schools that take care of the special-needs students. Even though in my community there were a bunch of public schools, they did not accept any special-needs students because they were not prepared to provide such services. The private school that I attended was very expensive and quite far away from my home. My dad had to pay the registration fee, bus expenses, costume, and books, as well as special equipment like a Braille Typer. To get to that school, I had to wake up too early to catch the bus. From first grade all the way up until fourth grade, my mom and I used to go out to wait for the bus. I had to be outside waiting, regardless of whether it was cold or hot. I am talking about a time like 5:30 in the morning.

In the winter, we used to stand under the umbrella to shelter from the rain! One time, the bus was very late due to the traffic. When it arrived, I was wet from head to toe. My backpack got all wet also. I started crying because I had all my Braille books in it! I worried also about the fact that teachers might scream at me, even though it was not my fault. I felt so devastated. When I arrived at school, I entered the classroom and my heart was beating fast. I sat on my little desk and I put my backpack near the heater to dry before the teachers arrived. Unfortunately, I was not lucky. Everybody arrived ten or fifteen minutes later! They all looked at me and said, "Khodr, what is this?"

When I tried to explain, one of them cut me off and said, "You better go home! You cannot use those books! So what are you planning to do?"

I started to cry! I didn't want to ruin my reputation at school. Suddenly, something made me feel powerful and led me to stand up and say to their faces, "You are my teachers, but this does not give you the right to humiliate me! I will not accept that! I tried to explain, although it does not need any farther explanation! You see the weather outside!"

The teachers got frustrated! They threatened me saying, "It is time to see the supervisor!"

They thought I would be scared and that I would back down, but instead I said, "Yes! Yes! This is exactly what I want! Take me there right now!"

One of the teachers pulled me roughly and took me to the supervisor's office. We waited for several minutes. When she finished all her work, she came toward me and said, "What's wrong Khodr? I know that you are one of the most respectful and smart students at our school."

I stood as a symbol of respect and said, "I was waiting for my bus this morning and I got wet with my backpack because it was raining hard very early this morning. The teachers got mad at me, and they know that it is not my fault." The supervisor calmed me down and told me that she would take care of it, and she sent me back to my classroom.

In the summertime, it was a bit easier. At least, the sun shines so early, but this did not do me any good. In Lebanon, there are a lot of stray dogs and cats. They are just living off garbage in the streets. They are not used to seeing anyone that early in the morning. So of course, I cannot see them, and I used to get very confused. One time, when my mother was not feeling well, I told her that I would wait by myself! Three dogs came toward me, and they started barking so loud, I got so scared. I did not know how to defend myself. I decided not to run away. This was something I had trouble with all the time. The dogs were about to touch me when I made a wild swift kick and, with good luck I think, I hit one of the dogs in the head. The rest ran away. In this way, I resolved this problem.

As I think back on those times, many of my problems seem to be related to that school bus in one way or another. On my way home, I used to arrive to my house at two in the afternoon. This was the time when the streets in Beirut have heavy pedestrian traffic. In addition, a lot of cars and motorcycles were crazily going back and forth. In many cases, motorcycles were about to hit me while I was getting out of the bus. Inches used to separate me from deadly accidents. I truly hated school just because of the trips in the mornings and afternoons. I felt that nothing was okay!

WHY CAN'T THEY UNDERSTAND?

I used to forget about everything that happened with me on my way to school as soon as I stepped into the school building. However, I had my other educational challenges inside the classroom. I did not have any advanced equipment available. I totally understood that Lebanon had inadequate services and facilities for the visually impaired students. My most powerful ally was Braille. Braille is a form of language that consists of raised dots used by blind individuals. I used the Braille Writer, which is a very traditional writing tool that has no other features. I used it along with the Braille books all year long. It was tough. I was the only Braille user in the classroom. My classmates were visually impaired, but most of them had enough vision that they were able to read print. I had to do many activities differently. Math and Science were the most complicated subjects. First, many of the diagrams were not accessible. Number charts, for example, were not an option for me because they were not represented in Braille. I used to memorize the entire thing. In other cases, I used to wait longer after the regular school day to get help from my friends or anyone who could help. Sometimes my friends had higher grades just because they had better opportunities. I hated myself because of my limitations! I thought it was not fair at all, but I had to live with it. There were no other choices.

One of the most obnoxious things that I truly hated back during all school years was the visitors. Occasionally, a group of students and their teachers would come and visit us. They wanted to know how we learn. I felt as if I were living on a different planet because some of them used to ask us questions that I considered senseless. One of the students asked me, "How do you get around?" I considered it a logical question because Lebanon is not prepared to be accommodating to the visually impaired. I told him, "I have a good memory; I know where I am at. Sometimes I have to ask for help!" What made me really so angry was this question from one of the other students: "I would like to know how you guys eat." I told her impatiently, "The same way you do."

VISUALLY IMPAIRED BUT NOT DISABLED

I spent eight years in that school. That trip was full of challenges and conflicts, but I became stronger. I used to find solutions to my problems on my own. This made me very creative! For example, I suggested an idea that would facilitate my work during the laboratory time. I told the Chemistry teacher that I wanted to see her after class. During this time, I was thinking about my idea very carefully because I wanted it to be successful! After the class was over, she came to my desk.

"How I can help you Khodr?" she asked me.

"I do not need any help, actually. But I have a great idea for you," I replied.

"I am listening!" She said.

"I would love to be a part of your lab work. So I thought about a good method for that. I came up with this picture in my mind. It is about a measuring tube that will be connected to an electronic horn. It has a cursor on a horizontal ruler that has on it the measurement in Braille and print," I explained. "My actual part in the lab experiment would be where I need to pour the liquid into the tube. I spot the cursor right next to the amount needed. I start pouring. When I reach the requested level, the horn will beep by itself notifying me that I have the desired amount."

"Oh my God, Khodr! It is a wonderful idea! It will be great!" She was thrilled by the idea!

The next day, I gathered a group of my friends. I presented the idea in front of them. They loved it! Every one of us took a part in the preparations. I bought several things! Other friends did the same. I had a friend who was very good at building things. It was his responsibility to make this idea a reality. As soon as everything was provided, we gave it to him. He started building it. He finished it in a matter of seven days. We tried it, and it worked well.

It was time to show it to the Chemistry teacher. We set up a meeting and we called our teacher to come over. When she saw what we did and how it worked, she was very surprised!

"Wow! Khodr, did you guys make it that fast?" she asked.

"Yes! I got a good brain and good ideas," I answered.

"It is obvious," she responded. This was quite an accomplishment for me. I started to be part of the lab activities. I felt that I was useful and I could be very productive.

OUT AND ABOUT

The society was a challenge also. People on the streets and neighbors, for example, would want to know what was wrong with me. A lot of them did not try to figure things out in a reasonable way. Rather, they used to make fun of me. One day, I was walking on the street. I was on my way to the store. I have a very good memory. It was very crowded! Cars were everywhere! Motorcycles were more than the people that were on the road going in all directions! Suddenly, a group of boys passed by, and they were planning to do something bad to me. Even though I did not see them, I was sure of it from the way they talked. I avoided them. They thought that they were smarter than I was. I entered a store with two doors that opened to two parallel streets. I went inside the store from one door and the boys waited outside. I escaped from the back-door that took me to the other side. I felt that I did not belong in that area. Everybody looked at me as if I were an alien. The way people used to treat me made me feel that I was not welcomed in this world. For instance, when my mom and I went shopping or something and we saw someone that my mother knew, that person pointed toward me asking about my disability without saying a word. Using signs or their lips they asked, "What's wrong with him? God help you!" They thought that I did not realize that! Because of that, I decided to go out more with my parents. I did not want them to get affected by what others say, but people kept on asking questions: "Does he attend any type of school? Is he smart?" or "Why do you spend so much money on him if it is going to end up for nothing?" I was not able to hold myself when I heard such remarks. One day I looked at our neighbor who asked similar questions and told him, "Hey! Do you think you are perfect? I challenge you to walk all over the area at night. You can tell me which store to stop at, and I will show you who is the smarter and braver." He laughed sarcastically, "You will be the winner!"

WHO IS SMARTER?

Many people believed that I was just another family member. I had nothing to do with my life except eat and sleep. I did my best to put an end to this resentful assumption. I started to go out a lot! I did not really care what people said or did. I used to spend my time in the cafe at night! I thought that I had nothing to lose anymore. I wanted to live like anybody else. I started to meet people from different ages and points of view. We talked and we discussed various matters. I tried my best to educate all the coffee drinkers and the cafe customers regarding disabled individuals. In one of our gatherings, I asked those who were present what they thought about disabilities. Some of them stood and said, "I think that disabled people must be like anybody else! They just need some extra help." I liked what he said. Another person added, "But in our country the disabled cannot be that independent because the culture is not all that accommodating." I did not interfere because I was enjoying the discussion. Their opinions were logical. The discussion was very interesting, and other people stepped right into it.

One person came toward me and said, "Disabled people must be all in one school. They should not let them go out. They are nothing but a headache." To show him that I had more education than he had, I asked him a question about science and the human body.

"What is the smallest bone in the human body?"

"Ha, ha, ha. That is so easy! Obviously, the answer is the toe," he replied with confidence.

"No sir! You are absolutely wrong," I said.

"No way," he responded in anger. I told him I'd give him another chance. I asked him about the official language in Brazil.

"Are you kidding me? Spanish! They speak Spanish," he hurried to say.

"Not at all. That is not their official language." He sat down on the chair. Then I asked him, "What do you think about people who have all their physical abilities, but aren't knowledgeable enough to know that Portuguese is the official language of Brazil? Are they superior to the handicapped that are nevertheless smart enough to know that the smallest bone in the body is the stapes of the middle ear? Who is the real headache here?" He paused for a bit and said, "Whatever." I paid him no further attention, but I showed the rest in that gathering that even though they could see, this did not mean that they were smarter. I kept doing the same in every place I went. I had to do that so people could accept me for who I am. They needed proof, and I provided that for them.

WHEN ALL HELL BROKE LOOSE

I used to wait for the summertime to come so I could get away from the city and its drama. Each summer, my family and I would drive out of the city up toward Baalbek to a village where we stayed. I enjoyed nature and the calmness of the place. I used to sit on the porch listening to the birds singing and the water falling from the spring in the pond in the garden. I loved smelling the fresh bread from the nearby bakery. I wished we could stay in the village. This calm and quiet was soon shattered. In July of 2006, I began to hate that place a lot. Thirty-three days of terror arrived with the Israeli warplanes. I lived through some very scary days. I was the first one to hear the warplanes coming toward the area.

"They came! They came!" I screamed from inside the house.

I knew that their presence was not good news for my people and me! They brought with them blaring sounds from bombs that destroyed little homes. They brought with them death to humans, animals, and plants. Not wanting to hear the Israelis war planes, I sat inside the house away from the windows.

"What shall we do?" I asked my parents.

"We can do nothing! We just need to be patient and hopefully all of this will be over soon." I did take their call. I mean, there was no other choice.

The fire trucks, mobile hospitals, and their staff were all over the place trying to rescue the victims. I cannot forget when I heard people screaming,

"Fire! Our house is on fire and our baby is in her bed sleeping!" To me that was very scary. I started to imagine this would happen to me. If it did, I would not know what to do. I did not really understand what was going on during that war. People who were able to see were running away. I did not know where to run. I was so frustrated. I did not know which spot was the safest. Could you imagine being blind and everyone near you is so helpless? Exactly! I had to help myself. I stayed in a five-room house with about seventy individuals. Most of them were children. It was noisy inside the house and outside! In all this chaos, I used to go with my dad to wait in line to get food. We had to wait very long and sometimes go back empty-handed. Basic life necessities were missing because everything was shut down. On our way back home, I could smell blood everywhere along with fire and dust. My dad described to me everything he saw.

"Here is the playground where you used to watch your friends playing soccer. It is all destroyed. This is one of the buildings that are completely leveled to the ground," he explained. "Nothing was saved!"

Nights were not peaceful either. People were as confused as I was. I did not deserve that life. Even here, in the place where I thought I would be safe and comfortable, there was no safety.

DRAMATIC CHANGE IN MY LIFE

The years 2007 and 2008 passed quickly. They were just like the previous years. Thankfully, by 2009 I finished grade eight and I was about to be in the ninth grade when a tremendous change happened in my life. My dad decided to immigrate to America. He thought about my future. He knew that in Lebanon I would not have the opportunity to fulfill my dreams. My dad made this decision because he thought about my long-term goals. All my friends got jobs! I could not get one! Even the high schools were not that helpful. I wondered if going to America would be useful. I wondered if I would be experiencing the same hardships but in a different place. In addition, my dad thought about the long-term consequences. I would not be able to get a job even if I got my Ph.D. I need a person with powerful connections to squeeze me in a workplace or something like that.

We were sitting in the living room when we heard my dad said, "No! It is not the right thing to stay here."

We asked him about what he meant!

"We better try to immigrate to America. The kids will have a better future, especially if they like school. They will get what they deserve there. No one will bother them! They will have opportunities."

In 2009, we immigrated to America. It was a very different environment. The language was different. Social customs were different as well. Beside the regular challenges, I had to take care of my special needs. Within three weeks, I was registered in school. I lived in Dearborn, but I had to go to Lincoln Park High School because the visually impaired program and services were located in Lincoln Park. I still remember the first day of school very distinctly. I was sitting in the living room at 6:45 in the morning anxiously waiting for my bus. When it arrived, I headed out. The driver's assistant helped me a little because there were several steps in the bus. I greeted everybody and I took a seat. On my way there, many questions came to my mind. How will the school be? Am I going to be satisfied? I was really hoping to get what I was thinking of.

Ten minutes later, the bus parked, and the driver said, "Okay! We are here! I will see you guys in the afternoon!"

When we got out of the bus, I did not know where to go or who to ask. I was like a lost person in a big dark forest! I was not scared though. I learned to have confidence in myself. I entered the building, and one of the staff stopped me and said, "Good morning! You are a new student, I bet! I have never seen you before. How I can help you?"

In my broken English, I answered, "Good morning! Yes, that is true. This is the first day of school for me. Could you please guide me to the visually impaired classroom?" I was happy because she understood me. My English was very limited at that time.

"Sure young man! I will take you there. Do you want to follow me? Or, you prefer to take my elbow?" she said.

"I will follow you. Thanks a lot!" I said. On our way to the visually impaired (VI) classroom, I was able to get a quick idea about the structure of the building. We were going through many hallways, and there were many students.

"Here we go sir," she said. We entered the room.

"Welcome, Khodr," the teacher said.

"Hello!" I said it in a very low voice. I was nervous. I still had not figured out exactly what my situation would be after that day. I sat on the chair, and the teacher started to introduce all the things they do.

"This classroom is for you to come and to get the help you need. We have several computers that are supported with screen readers. A screen reader is a program that is designed to read everything written on the computer monitor. It is not perfect, but it helps a lot! Also, we use the Braille Note Apex. Apex is an electronic Braille machine. It gives the blind student the opportunity to be independent, successful, and productive. We have a teacher who will come and show you how to operate it. Moreover, we use the CD player. This piece of technology is used to play your books. Some books are available on the CD for you, so you could listen to them. It has so many features," she explained.

"Wow!" I stood there speechless. I had not seen or heard anything like this in Lebanon. I had better excel, I thought. She continued her introduction, "Any new student has to be evaluated. There are several tests that you must take, and your grades will decide your level."

"Okay!" I said. I was slightly worried because my English was not that good yet. Then, the teacher took me and showed me the different places in the building, such as the cafeteria, gym, restroom, etc. She did all the paperwork. The test was scheduled for the following day. When the school day was over, I felt that I had achieved something. I brushed all my fears away. I was now more comfortable.

On the next day, I arrived to the school! I was so ready for the test. I went all by myself to the classroom. No one had to show me how to go. I entered the room. No one was there. Five minutes later, the teacher came.

"Good morning! You are early! Are you ready for the test?" she asked.

"Yes, sure!" I replied. We went to the test room. The test consisted of reading, writing, listening, and speech. I took the reading test first. It was not that hard, actually. I had some trouble speaking and communicating, but other than that, I think that it was a fairly good exam. A week later, all the results came out. I did not do too badly at all.

"Yeah! You will be in the mainstream classes," she said jovially.

"Great start," I said.

I started with five classes. I did really well, but being in class with other sighted students was something that I was not used to. Also, there were about thirty-five students in every single class. I was the only blind student in each class. I was the only one who used a computer in that class. I received my work from my teachers through email. I got all that I needed. In some cases, I received my work in Braille. Teachers sent the worksheets to the title VI classroom where it was embossed, and I loved it. Teachers were cooperative. My classmates were helpful too. They showed me some additional things in the building. They helped me in the visual parts of the homework. Also, they helped me in reading the stories and novels. I built many friendships in a month. I was like a social butterfly. Talking to many of my classmates was a great opportunity for me to get to know the language and the culture. I took many parts in celebrating the American holidays. I hung out with my friends a lot. We went to all kinds of places and activities such as sports, movies, and restaurants. No one made me feel that I was blind. I liked the environment. I was astonished by the respect that I got from everybody. I was enjoying every single minute of my high school years. Furthermore, a mobility teacher showed me how to move around properly. At first, she introduced the white cane.

"This is called the white cane. It is colorful. Blind individuals use it as identification just so others know."

I liked the idea. It is very protective. I used it outside the building to practice using it. I learned how to catch the public bus. I was fearless. Crossing Fort Street in Lincoln Park was like a piece of cake for me. I was very satisfied and I knew the area very well.

Those years flew by super fast. I established an excellent record. I learned how to operate all the adaptive technology quickly and received many academic achievement awards. I was honored several times by local organizations, and most importantly, I graduated on time with a 4.0 grade point average.

In August 2012, I began attending Henry Ford College (HFC). Based on my grades in high school, as well as the frequent community service programs I have engaged in over the years, I was selected for the Bridge Program between Henry Ford and the University of Michigan, which practically guarantees my acceptance at University of Michigan-Dearborn if I find my academic major there. I am about to get an Associate Degree in Pre-Special Education at HFC in the winter semester of 2015. Everything is on the right track. I am getting what I have been planning for and I believe that hard work pays off.

Welcome to the Boo

Jeffrey Koscielny

September 11, 2001, was a day that changed the way we lived in our secure and peaceful world where we only dreamed about the good things in life. On CCN, we watched planes crash into the World Trade Center in New York City, then the Pentagon in Washington, D.C. Over three thousand lives were lost that day. Our feeling that no one would try to attack the United States of America changed that day. For several days, people were glued to the TV sets trying to get any information they could to be reassured everything would go back to normal. I stopped at the bar to watch the news and have a beer. Like everyone else, I was staring in disbelief as the World Trade Center came crashing down. My friend Chet was working behind the bar that day.

"Jeff, here's a beer on me. What do you think about this shit?" he asked.

"I do not know, Chet, but I think I am going to war, my friend," I said.

"Jeff, I think you're right. Good luck," Chet said as he looked at me.

"This is going to be a long war," I said.

Two years after 9/11, my National Guard unit received orders for deployment to Iraq. As I said to Chet, I was going to war. This is one soldier's story of adventure and danger and the long trip to hell that the world came to know as *Abu Ghraib Prison*.

103

☆☆☆

My unit reported to Selfridge Air National Guard Base (SANGB) on December 7, 2004, for active duty and deployment to Iraq. We stayed at SANGB for four days then flew to Fort Bliss, Texas for 8–10 weeks of training. The night before we left, the Michigan National Guard had a big sendoff for us. Our families came to hear speeches, watch us in formation, and see us one last time. After we were released, we went to dinner one last time and said our goodbyes. After our families left, we started to form our new families from among the soldiers we would be with for one year. We would live, eat, sleep, and die with the soldiers in our company. We formed into our sections and started drinking beer and hard liquor until it was time to leave.

We left Michigan to a fate unknown. Still hungover from the night before, we landed in Fort Bliss. We drove for a fifty-mile trip to a range outside of Fort Bliss in the middle of the desert. We unloaded trucks filled with our gear, weapons, and personal bags to our barracks. The barracks we moved into had not been used in ten years, and they were filthy. Designed to hold ninety men, we fit one hundred forty-five soldiers with their gear in an H-style barrack: two long legs that were the living area connected in the middle by the bathroom and laundry room. Down the sides were rows of bunk beds. Running down the middle were our weapons that ranged from M-4s to heavy machine guns. I shared a bunk space with our medic, Doc Johnston. He had the bottom bed, and I had the top. Doc was from the west side of the state. He was about twenty-six years old with blond hair and blue eyes. He was always upbeat and smiling. Doc and I had known each other for about eight years; he had been in the unit for about 10 years. He was married with one kid and a very pretty wife. After we unloaded all our gear, we bedded down for the night; not a lot of small talk, just some good sleep. The next morning we went to the chow hall: a big circus tent that served UGR (unit group rations). These were pre-packed eggs, ham, and bacon or sausage patties. Everything was served out of preheated tins, except toast and cereal. We received two hot meals a day: breakfast and dinner. Lunch was meal ready to eat (MRE) bag army lunch. For sixty days, we did our medical records checks, shots, and more shots, covering everything from A to Z. We were also shooting weapons that included M-4s, heavy machine guns, grenade launchers, and everything else to kill the bad guys. We covered everything from roadside bombs to patrolling tactics, room clearing, and manning check points. Everything we learned was right from the book because no one was back from the invasion yet. We were their relief.

Our company was an airborne LRRS (long-range surveillance company) consisting of one hundred forty-five soldiers broken down into five platoons of twenty-five to thirty-eight soldiers. The line platoons consisted of six teams of six soldiers, one platoon sergeant, and a platoon leader. The communication platoon had five base stations of five soldiers and their communication gear mounted on Humvees. The operation platoon was the brain trust of the company for doing all the planning and controlling the movement of all the units at one time. Their job was to know where everyone was at all times and to have backup for the soldiers if they needed help. After sixty days of training and boredom, we finally moved to the airfield and waited to be transported to Iraq. The move took place on February 15. One hundred forty-five personnel with vehicles and gear were moving closer to the aircraft that would fly us over to "the sandbox." Four aircrafts flew our equipment and us. The manifests were made out so that certain key elements were not on the same aircraft in case they were shot down. My aircraft was due to fly out on February 21, 2004, one day after my birthday. What a hell of a birthday present that was. When we found out where we were going, we had a hard time. We drew our live rounds, 12 magazines of 5.56 ball ammunition for our M-4 carbines, rounds for the M-60 machines guns, and AT4 anti-tank rounds. I spent two days arranging my gear, body armor, and ammo pouches in the right place and making sure my magazines would fit into my M-4. I loaded my backpack with smokes, books, toilet articles, a change of clothes, and anything else I thought I would need to live on for 36 hours. The hard part was waiting for the flight, making last-minute phone calls to the loved ones back home to tell them that I loved them and I would do well in Iraq. I sat in silence thinking to myself "what if" this and "what if" that. The only thing I knew was I did not want to let comrades down.

NO ONE GETS LEFT BEHIND

February 19, 2004, that night was a perfect Texas evening about 60 degrees. A soft wind was blowing off the mountains that ran down from the north border to Mexico. I was sitting outside enjoying the evening, drinking a coke, when my friend Eric showed up. He sat down next to me and asked, "Hey, Jeff, you okay?"

"Yeah, just worried about my guys that left on the flights before me, and tomorrow is my birthday," I said.

"Cool!" he said as he pulled out a pint of Jack Daniels. "Here is to you," he added as he opened the bottle and took a shot.

"Thanks," I said, and then I took a shot too.

"You scared, Jeff?" he asked.

"No, just did not want to let anyone in the unit down. How about you, Eric?" I asked.

"I trained for this for many years, and now it's my time to see if I could cut the mustard," he answered.

Eric was a team leader in one of the line platoons with five people under him. It was his responsibility to get them there and back in one piece.

"Here's a shot, Jeff, to your birthday."

"Same to you, my friend," I said as I took one too. We killed the pint and walked back to the tent in total silence. We did not say a word. We just looked up at the clear sky.

"Eric, I'll see you in the morning. Ya take care, my brother," I said as I left him.

0600 we awoke for chow. Same stuff: eggs, bacon, hash browns, and coffee. I was with Eric, eating and bitching about the chow, when we found out we had to be at the airfield at 1630 that day.

"Jeff, happy birthday," Eric said as he gave me a hug and then started laughing.

"F— off," I said jokingly. "You are an old f—ing man now," I added as I flipped him the bird. I went back to my bunk, rechecked my gear, helmet, body armor, mags, and my backpack. I cleaned my M-4 for the last time. At about 1200 Eric, Matt, and about 10 other guys came to my bunk bringing a Hostess cupcake with a candle in it.

"Happy birthday, old man," Eric said and started singing happy birthday. I stood up and just smiled, then told all of them to go f— themselves. Matt gave me a big hug, and we all shook hands like it was another day. At 1630 we loaded buses for the airfield. Each bus had 36 guys on a one-way trip; the only way home was to walk off the plane or get carried off

107

on a stretcher or in a coffin. We sat in the terminal waiting for final manifest call (calling all 36 names that were to be on the plane heading to uncertainty). We were flying at 20:00 hours. Many of us went outside to smoke for about an hour, looking at the mountains, engaging in small talk, and just thinking about the upcoming events. At 1900, we were told to grab our gear and move to the aircraft. I picked up my gear and fell in line as we walked out to the aircraft. We loaded through the front door, making our way to the back and throwing our packs on our vehicles that we were flying over with us too. Up the stairs to the passengers' seats on the upper deck, with my interceptor body armor (IBA) and my weapon, I sat next to Popp, a guy who had been in the unit for about four years.

"You ready old man?" Popp said.

"Go f— yourself," I said and he just laughed. We took off at 2000. Our next stop was Moran, Spain. We laid up for about 8 hours, then we flew on to Balad, Iraq for a year of hell. After a fourteen-hour flight, we arrived in Spain for a short layover. We heard we had about 8 hours before we would load up and fly to Iraq. My friend Matt and I went to the coffee shop to have some coffee. Little did we know that it was a Mediterranean espresso place. In the inside, it was just old wooden tables and chairs. Smoked hams hung from the rafters along with other meat products. Since it was Matt's birthday that day, we had an espresso to celebrate him turning twenty-four. A few other guys from our chalk (a group of soldiers that deploy from a single aircraft) showed up too. We just sat, drank coffee, and bulled about what was up ahead. About four hours later, we headed back to the terminal to load our aircraft. At 1030, we took off for Balad, Iraq. It was an airbase about fifty miles north of Baghdad, the main staging area for incoming troops. About one hour out, the crew chief started putting on his body armor. I looked at Popp and said, "What the hell is going on?"

"Guess we better do it," Popp retorted.

"The last time we landed, the aircraft took fire," the crew chief said.

I had never seen people move so fast putting on gear, helmets, and flak jackets, then calmly sit back down waiting for the worst to happen. The pilot put the plane in a steep dive from 10,000 feet to about 1,000 feet in about one minute. He called it a combat landing. He leveled off at 500 feet. We finally hit the runway with a hard bounce. When he put the engines in reverse to slow down the air speed, we jumped forward in our seats as we taxied to the area where we were supposed to unload without knowing what was ahead of us. When we stopped, the chief said, "Welcome to Iraq and good luck. Now get off his aircraft."

As we made our way downstairs, we could see the tail of the plane starting to open so we could drive our vehicles off. The Air Force soldiers wanted us off the plane ASAP because they did not want to stay on the ground for long. We hopped in our vehicles and drove off the plane to a holding area where we met soldiers from the other flights. The first thing we did was to go to a briefing tent to get our ID cards swiped saying that we were in the country. We headed to our sleeping quarters in tent city. We made our bunks with just sleeping bags and our packs for pillows because we had been awake for about fourteen hours straight from the time we landed in Spain until we landed in Iraq. At about 0700 we woke up to see about 90 guys from our company who landed the day before we did. I ran into my buddy Matt from my platoon.

"How you been, Jeff? Let's go get some chow," Matt said.

"How was your flight?" I asked as we walked to breakfast.

"Okay, same as yours, I guess."

We made our way to the chow hall. It was just about four mobile homes put side by side where we went in one way and out the other. We had breakfast then headed out back to the area where we were the night before to get our vehicles ready to convoy south to our new home, the prison at Abu Ghraib. We loaded our vehicles with sandbags on the floor, a M249 Squad Automatic Weapon (SAW) of 1,000 rounds on the top turret, a SAW on the left side, and a M203 grenade launcher on the right side. I was the tank commander (TC), Clark was the gunner, Bob was on the left side, and Matt was on the right side. The convoy brief was simple: watch out for improvised explosive devices (IED). If you get hit, return fire and get out of the kill zone. Our objective was the prison 50 miles south of Balad. It was about a 2–3 hour drive, provided that nothing happened. We were supposed to leave at 0900 the next day. Wake up at 0600, go eat chow, grab some coffee, pack your gear, and load up for the drive south. In our convoy we had five gun trucks, three five tons with our gear, and about 90 soldiers locked, loaded, and ready for bear.

As we pulled out of the airbase, the mood was okay. We thought, since we are here, let's get it done. Time to kick some ass. The drive was down a two-lane road lined with the junk of war on both sides: burned-out trucks, tanks, and automobiles. The local Iraqi people set up stands on the side of the road to sell water, fruits, or meat in mud huts with an open front. They were just trying to make a living, but we saw them as enemies trying to kill us. We eyed everyone with a bad feeling. They made one wrong move and they were dead. After about two hours, we hit the main highway running south. It was a nice three-lane highway with a median between the north and southbound lanes. Off to our right, we could see the prison in the middle of nowhere, as if it was saying, "Do not come here. Drive on. Keep going." The prison had walls about ten feet high and about three feet wide. This gruesome-looking place became our home for the next year. We made a left turn over the median into the front gate, calling out over the radio that we would pass the checkpoint when we entered the prison heading to our living area. The place looked sad. The buildings were burned-out, and the soldiers wore blank stares on their faces as if they were saying, "Thank God, you are here. Now we can go home."

WELCOME TO HELL

Abu Ghraib was built between 1950 and 1960. At first, it was an insane asylum, then a prison, and finally it became Saddam Hussein's torture chamber. The word Abu refers to "father" in Arabic, and Ghraib has been interpreted to mean "strange." To the locals, the prison became known as the house of strange fathers, and to the Americans, the biggest disgrace in recent times. As we rolled into the compound, the first thing we saw was a large wasteland of nothing but empty sand, blown-up trees, and the smell of shit. The prison was a one-mile by one-mile area surrounded by a wall that was 12 feet high, with guard towers placed every 50 meters. There were four living support areas (LSA), one hardstand prison, and two open prison areas. The LSAs were prison blocks with walls around them. They looked like small castles on the vast desert floor. They were complete with six guard towers and two gates one on the east end and one on the west end. Inside the walls

111

were ten buildings connected by one long corridor that ran the length of the compound and branched off into the buildings. The buildings had two floors with prison cells, an open bay, a doorway leading to the exercise yard, and one leading to the main corridor. The cells had wood covering the front and housed three soldiers sleeping on cots arranged in a U-shaped pattern with their gear under their cots.

Since we had arrived on different aircrafts, we drove to the prison on different convoys. We were finding our platoons and teams to be complete again. After I unloaded my gear, Clark and I went to the rest of our team.

"Hey, Sgt. K. This place looks like a f—ing shit hole," Clark said.

"Hell yeah. It's done. What? You think we were going to the Ritz? Come on, let's find Nannie," I said turning around and looking at him. As we entered our cellblock, we found Nannie, Chad, and Charlie grinning like they had just hit the lottery.

"What do you think about your new home?" Chad asked.

"Not bad. It beats the tents we had at Balad," I said as I looked at Clark. Chad grabbed Clark's gear, taking him to the cell he shared with Jeff and other soldiers in our platoon. Bob grabbed my gear and said, "Come, Serge, here is your cell. How was the drive down?"

"Not bad. Peaceful, no contact, kind of boring, I shared a cell with Ski and Bomber, two team leaders from my platoon. My cell was on the long leg of the U. How you been? Did everything go okay?" I asked Bob.

"Yeah, been here about three days; the chow sucks, but you are safe inside the building. I have my own cell, call it the whack shack, put my pinups on the wall. Everything is cool."

112

I just smiled and shook my head laughing to myself, knowing what he meant.

My team was composed of four guys. Charlie was the oldest at 45 and had been in for 20 years in the Guard. He was a back fill and came from another unit just before we left. Chad was 20 and fresh out of the Army. He joined the Guard in the summer of 2003, spent his time in Korea, and said he was moving back after we were done. Clark was 21, joined in December of 2002. He had never been away from home, much less being sent overseas. Nannie was 20. He joined up in the summer of 2003. He was a computer wizard who liked to hunt deer and to watch porn movies.

At 1700 we put our IBA and helmets on and we walked to the chow hall that was in the middle of the compound. This was made of a group of buildings about 700 meters from our LSA. The chow hall was run by a British contractor who knew how to cook food his way, not the American way. His British menu contained meat, stale bread, brown salad, luke-warm coffee with milk, and no desserts of any kind. We stacked our weapons, IBA, and helmets along the side of the wall and walked to the servicing line to grab our chow on to the salad bar, before we went to get our drink of choice. We sat at tables and chairs that were too small. They reminded me of my years back in grade school. After we were done, we grabbed a cup of Joe to-go and made our way back to the LSA for the night to find out what was going on the next day.

Abu Ghraib Prison was located twelve miles west of Baghdad and fifteen miles east of Al Fallujah in the heart of the Sunni Triangle. This city was the scene of some of the worst fighting in Iraq. On both corners of the prison were two mosques: one for the Sunnis and one for the Shiites. These mosques could look right down onto the compound. The

113

prisoners would be watching our every move. Working in the prison, there were 1,000 Americans divided up between medical personnel, military police, marines, and us to guard 7,000 prisoners ranging from high-value targets to everyday people. Our unit was assigned two mission tower guards. We had to watch the outside and the inside of the prison at the same time. The other mission was convoy escort. This involved driving up and down the highway protecting supply trucks to the airport. The route we drove was called Route Tampa, known as the highway to hell due to the numerous IEDs and ambushes. We drove that route three times a week with three supply trucks and four to five gun trucks, picking up supplies and personnel from the airport. The airport was fifteen miles from the prison. Each trip took twenty minutes up to four hours, depending on what we had to deal with. Inside the prison, we had boredoms, mortars, rocket attacks, and small firearm attacks to put up with. The plan of the Iraqis who were fighting us was to try to knock down the outer walls of the prison so the prisoners could escape. The random attacks killed more prisoners than Americans. Every day, right after the call to pray, we had to go to a handstand building to seek cover. At one point in time, we were being hit 4–6 times a day. Other times, we could see rockets flying over our heads on the way to the green zone (Baghdad). Our day was the same routine: wake up, eat chow, pull our 4–6 hour guard shift, improve our area, clean weapons, and get ready for convoys the next day.

On one of the convoys, and these were daily, we had to escort our supply truck that was driven by my friend Ken and his gunner Steve. In my truck, I had Chris on the gun, Bob sitting behind me, and John was my driver. We joined the convoy at 0700 to do our final prep and the convoy briefing. In the convoy, there were six supply trucks and five gun trucks commanded by a female military police sergeant. Her briefing was quite simple: drive fast and if we are hit, return fire, drive through the ambush, and shoot anything that looks like a bad guy. We pulled out of the prison with her truck in the lead. She was followed by two supply trucks, a gun truck, two more supply, then gun truck, two more supply trucks, and the last was a gun truck to bring up the rear. Our truck drove in front of Ken so we could keep our eyes on him at all times in case he was engaged with small arms fire. We hit the highway at a speed of 50–60 miles an hour. We were running like a bat out of hell, not stopping for anything. If there was a car in the way, we ran it off to the side. When we came to an overpass, we went in on the left and came out on the right to throw off any shooters that were on top of the bridge. The radio cracked as we passed checkpoints. We called up whenever we saw anything that looked like a target or anything that looked like an IED. After 20 minutes, we came to the narrow road leading to the airport. We cut across the median over the northbound lane on to the final four miles to safety. When we entered the gate we stopped, cleared our weapons, put them on safe, and then we drove to the parking lot. I stayed with our truck as my soldiers went to grab some chow from the Bob Hope mess hall. As they came back with a cup of coffee for me, they could not help but tell me how great it was. After we loaded up our trucks with water and food, the guys went to the PX (store) for basic stuff such as soap, books, and anything to help pass the time back at the prison. At 1400, we formed up at the staging area for the drive back. After the quick brief, we loaded our weapons and did a radio check between trucks and our command post back at the prison. We fell into our positions in convoy order and we drove out the gate down the narrow road to the highway.

We hit the highway at a slow speed waiting for the convoy to make the turn, then we picked up speed all the way up to 50 mph. About 10 miles down the road Chris saw a van trying to get on the freeway.

"Contact right 3 chock," Chris screamed.

We took our weapons off safe turning to the contact: a van trying to come on the freeway. I tried to wave him off first by hand signals, then by pointing my weapons at the van. While this was happening, a person popped his head and body out the passenger side window.

"Hold your fire. Hold your fire!" I yelled. We had the van in our sights waiting to pull the trigger, and then the person went back into the van. A few seconds later, he popped out again.

"There he is. He has something in his hand!" Chris yelled.

"Hold your fire. Wait for my command!" I yelled.

When he came out again, he had two melons in his hands to show us that he was friendly. The van finally came to a stop. We searched it and the people who were on it and made sure it was safe before we left. As we drove, we were still watching the van and gripping our weapons tightly. We all put our weapons on safe for the last five miles to the prison, our home. As the massive walls of the prison loomed up, we let out a deep breath that we did not have to shoot up the van. We pulled into the prison, cleared our weapons, and then drove to our command post. As we parked the truck and began to climb out, everyone was soaked in sweat. Chris looked at me and said, "Jeff, I was going to whack the van, man."

"It's cool, man. You did your job. The guy was just trying to be friendly," I said. I went to check into the command post to tell the Operations Section we were back and nothing happened. As the soldiers were unloading the truck, Bob came up to me and said, "Man! I was scared as shit! That dude freaked me out."

"Hey, man. It's cool. He scared the shit out of me too. Go clean your weapon and get some down time," I said.

We did five more convoys to the airport before we found out forty-five personnel were heading up north to Mosul. We would be leaving in three days in a convoy of ten trucks. The rest would fly by chopper to Mosul.

The day came when Bob, Chad, John, and Charlie were in the convoy and I was flying up with 30 personnel leaving from the airport. We said our goodbyes.

"Be safe and see you when I get there," I said.

Two days later, we convoyed one last time to the airport to hook up with our birds for the flight to Mosul. As we drove out of the prison for the last time, I could not help but think about the soldiers we left behind. After thirty-five days in the prison, I was glad to be leaving. It was time for some new scenery and hopefully better chow. We stayed up north for ten months before going back to the airport near Baghdad for our flight back to Kuwait to become a company again. I did not see my friends until we reached Kuwait. Everyone had stories about the past year in Iraq: some good, some bad. Most of all, we just wanted to sleep, eat, and be safe.

Ten years later, April 12, 2014, we finally had a reunion of the guys who were in Iraq. About 50 showed up. There were many hugs for the guys. Some I had not seen in ten years. We drank, told stories, and joked like it was yesterday. We remembered things that happened a long time ago. We all were older, heavier, and some of us with gray, thinning hair. We were a band of brothers ten years ago, and now we still are, only ten years older.

Mistake of My Life

LaTosha Ballard

I remember the expression on my parents' faces when I came home and told them I was graduating a year early. The big hugs and kisses showed me they were extremely proud. It was a hot summer day in June, and here I was running around trying to finish final touches before leaving Henry Ford High School. Family and friends gathered at Cobo Arena to celebrate my joyous occasion. Afterwards, we went to Sweetwater Tavern for lunch. As lunch ended, everyone went his or her separate way. Thereafter, I hung out with friends at a few venues in downtown Detroit.

I was indecisive about whether to go to school or to work. With materialistic things being on my mind, I decided to work. Needless to say, my parents were infuriated with the decision I made. At that time, I felt like they wanted to live their lives through me. Having my own place and being independent was all that mattered. I gained employment at Wendy's and that lasted two years. It was an alright job because it paid bills and allowed me to sustain myself. I had a plan to work and attend trade school. After becoming certified as a Medical Assistant, I began looking for fulltime work at local hospitals and doctors' offices.

One day, during the search for full-time employment, I had a craving for some Chester Fried Chicken. After purchasing my meal, I ran across a man named James. We chatted briefly before we decided to exchange phone numbers. I shared my

119

dreams and desires with him, and it seemed like we had a lot in common. We kept in contact via phone for about a month before dating. He was a man that loved seeing and making his lady happy. I could ask him for anything, and he provided. What woman wouldn't want a nice-looking man who was a provider? James was tall, brown-skinned, and medium-built. He was clean cut and had the gift of gab. He was very charming and had my nose opened full force. We took road trips together, and he bought me a bevy of clothing and jewelry. I remember us driving to Miami to visit his cousin for a week. We enjoyed the night life, South Beach, and shopping. Even though we had a few disagreements during the trip, the fun I was having allowed me to push those thoughts to the back of my mind. I fell in love fast and I thought I had the perfect life. With a job and new man who was good to me, I thought I was on top of the world and things were peachy for me. Within a year, he asked me to move in with him, and I obliged.

One morning, I was rushing to the bathroom and I didn't know he was in there. The first thing I noticed was cocaine in three rows on the ledge of the bathtub. James was sitting on the toilet with dilated pupils and a blank look. I was devastated and alarmed by finding out he was getting high on his own supply. With all the questions I asked him about his habit and how long he'd been using, he gave me nothing. We didn't talk for a few days because I was angry and felt he betrayed me. How could I be betrayed by a man I was living with and in love with?

"Do you plan on getting help or do you want to call it quits?" I asked him.

"I'm a grown man, and I'm taking care of you," he said.

With tears in my eyes, I asked, "Why are you hurting yourself? Is this the way you want to live?"

120

"I'm not hurting myself, and quit talking to me about it because I don't want to hear it," he answered brusquely.

He assured me he would do the right thing because he didn't want me out of his life.

A few months later, I discovered I was pregnant. Excited about my bundle of joy, I couldn't wait to tell James and my family. I called him on his cell phone and asked, "Are you near the house? I have something to share with you."

"Tosha, can it wait until later? I'm busy." he replied.

"What's more important than your child growing inside me?" I responded in disappointment.

His entire demeanor and tone changed instantaneously.

"Baby, why didn't you tell me? How far are you?"

"I just found out. I'm around nine weeks."

"I'll be home shortly. We can grab a bite and talk."

"Ok, I can go for a corned beef. See you soon."

I remembered my grandmother telling me at an early age that the quickest way to get rid of a man was to tell him you were pregnant. I found out that she was right when I got into my second trimester. It didn't take long before he became the Grinch that Stole Christmas. I started seeing changes in him that I didn't like. He stayed away from home for nights at a time and he became mentally and physically abusive. I was young, and he thought he could tell me anything.

I became tired of him staying out all night messing around on me with different women. Women in our neighborhood started not liking me because of him. He was involved with a girl named Joy, and she hated my guts. I never did anything to her, but it was always something when I ran into her. I was ordering some food from McDonald's. When I knew that she was working at that place, I had a feeling that something bad was going to happen. Before I could pay for my food,

121

an employee informed me that Joy took my burgers and stepped on them with her feet. I became enraged and demanded to see her. As she came to the front, I asked her, "Is there a problem? Did you step on my burger and plan on selling it to me thinking that my baby and I were going to eat the food?" Unhappy with the response Joy had given me, I jumped over the counter and we began fighting. Had I been thinking reasonably, I should have reported her to the manager and demanded that they fire her after her disgusting act. Some patrons who were dining in jumped in to break up the fight. After the situation settled down, I explained to the manager what happened, and he decided that calling the police was unnecessary. They just asked me politely to leave the restaurant and made my food over again.

After I gave birth to our beautiful daughter, I decided it was time for us to move on with life without him. Of course, I wanted him to be involved with his daughter, but as far as our relationship went, I knew in my heart that it was over. How much could one take? I remember our home being raided by DPD (Detroit Police Department) because of his lifestyle. One day, there were four knocks at the door.

"Who is it?" I asked.

"Detroit Police Department. We have a search warrant. Open the door."

I was devastated and scared of what was going to happen next. In total, there were about ten cops inside our home destroying the place. They busted up walls and floors throughout the entire house. While this was taking place, Officer Reid asked if I could come into another bedroom.

"Yes, of course," I responded.

"How long has James been dealing out this house?" he asked.

"I knew he was using, but I am unaware of him distributing from the house because I worked during the day," I told him.

Noticing that I was shaking and tearing up, the officer became pleasant while questioning me.

"Do you have any priors?" he asked. No.

"I'd never been in trouble before," I emphasized.

"What are you doing with someone like James?" he asked.

"Sometimes you can't choose who you fall in love with," I told him.

After destroying everything in sight, they found less than fifty grams of heroin, one hundred twenty ecstasy pills, five pounds of marijuana, and a 9 mm firearm. James admitted to the officers that everything they found belonged to him and I had no knowledge of anything. They read him his Miranda rights and escorted him down to the Wayne County Jail. He took a plea and was sentenced to five years of probation.

Prior to that incident, he pulled his gun on me on several occasions when we had a disagreement. The scariest time was when I dropped my daughter off with my sister. My girlfriends didn't care for James, nor did he care for them. I tried to hang out with them at their house on my own time to keep confusion down. Janna wanted to pick me up for a night on the town. That particular day, I could tell he had been snorting cocaine because he kept rubbing his nose and making obnoxious noises with his throat. As I was getting dressed, he asked, "Where are you going?"

"Out with my girlfriend," I said. I was looking, feeling, and smelling like a million bucks.

"Did you drop my daughter off to go out?" he asked.

"Yes, for a few hours, and I was going to pick her up afterwards."

Dealing with his foolishness and my daughter on my own, I became burned out. I just needed to get away and forget about how my life was spiraling downwards. I was in the bathroom putting on makeup when he entered, yelling at me.

"Did you hear what I said? Go get my baby and bring her home."

"James, you're high and need to get out of my face. Janna and the other girls are on their way to pick me up."

Moments later, I felt his gun on the temple of my head. Screaming hysterically, I said "Get your gun off of me. I'm tired of you pulling it out. What's wrong with you? Would you draw it on me around our daughter? I couldn't hurt my daughter but can and will hurt you if you keep pushing me."

"Go get my daughter and don't you dare leave the house," he threatened. I began crying profusely, pleading with him not to kill me and to remove his gun from my head. I became depressed and couldn't believe the changes he was going through. After I spent half the day deciding what I was wearing out and after having done a manicure and pedicure, I called the girls and told them I became ill, and I went and picked my daughter up.

The final straw was when we went to have a barbecue at Belle Isle. I began telling him how unloved I felt and how I couldn't deal with our relationship anymore.

"Why do you feel like you can chastise me when I'm the mother of your child?" I asked him.

"You don't know your place," he replied.

"It's time for us to separate. Do you still want to be involved with your daughter?" I asked him.

"My baby ain't going nowhere and neither are you," he replied, as if he owned us. I remained calm and told him that when we got back home I was packing up and moving. He called me every name but the child of God. I remained calm and replied, "James, this isn't necessary. You'll be living single and you'll be doing whatever you like." I expressed to him how much I loved him and with time, maybe we could fix our relationship. I knew that I had a lot of healing to do before I could consider going back to James. After I wished him well with his life, he picked me up by my feet and put me in the trunk of his car. I was kicking and screaming for him to let me out. He tuned me out by turning up his radio system. I began saying my prayers because I was in desperate need of help, and the man upstairs was the only person I could depend on. About fifteen minutes later, he opened the trunk and let me out.

"Really, you hate me that much to suffocate me in your trunk?" I began walking off the island crying hysterically and trying to reach Jefferson Street. I was going to call anyone I could think of to pick me up. James started driving by me apologizing and begging me to get in the car. At this point, I was ignoring him as if he didn't exist.

A stranger drove up and asked, "Miss, are you okay? Can I give you a ride?"

"No, I'm fine. Thank you for asking," I replied. As James was still driving by me he said, "You better get in this car or else!" Not knowing if he was going to kill me or kill the stranger, I got in the car and let him take me home.

Once we got home, I called my best friend to pick my daughter up and I began packing up our belongings.

"You're not moving my child out of the house," he kept yelling after she was picked up. After I kept ignoring him, he smacked me, and we began fighting like cats and dogs. I thought this couldn't be life. I must be in a nightmare. Somehow, we ended up scuffling in the kitchen. "James, please let me go. I can't breathe," I begged.

With his tight grip around my neck, I began losing consciousness. I was feeling around the counter for an object to hit him so that he could release me. I managed to get ahold of a knife and I stabbed him with it. Unbeknown to me, someone called the police and ambulance. Here I was, trying to explain what happened to the police, but they weren't trying to listen to anything I was saying. The only thing they said to me was my Miranda rights. James was put on a stretcher and taken to Providence Hospital. After all the abuse this man inflicted upon me, they wanted to charge me with attempted murder. I've never been in any type of trouble, and they were trying to railroad me. I was jailed down in Oakland County for two weeks. It's a place I wouldn't wish on my enemy, nor could I allow my dog to live in. It was crowded, cold, and its atmosphere was disgusting. The only thing I wanted was to be released to go home to my daughter. The prosecutors wanted me to plead guilty to attempted murder, carrying up to twenty-five years in a state prison. I became very ill and disturbed because of their plan. The only thing I could do was to have a trial.

Having knowledge of the justice system, I knew I was going to have to retain a lawyer who specialized in criminal cases. During my stay in jail, all I could think about was how I let my parents and daughter down. I was in a messy situation, and it was hard to get out of it. I had mixed feelings and even became suicidal because I couldn't stomach being caged down twenty-five years. I was very prayerful and asked God to send me home to my child. I didn't care about the other losses I took. I just wanted to be home with my baby.

I had to put my thinking cap on fast and decided Mr. Harris was perfect for the job, even though I knew he was going to charge me an arm and leg for representing me. Mr. Harris was from the inner city, and he knew Detroit inside and out. He represented a few of my family members and friends. I was highly confident that he'd get the charges dropped because he went from working the streets as a narcotics officer, prosecutor, and now a criminal defense lawyer. One time, I went to give him a cashier's check for a relative.

"What made you go from a prosecutor to a defense lawyer?" I asked him.

"I had to shake hands with the devil to live better," he said.

I thought that was his honest answer. When the trial date came, I entered a crowded courthouse filled with strangers, family, and friends who came to hear my case. It was very embarrassing, and I felt outside myself. As beautiful as a person that I was, I was fighting for my life. The only thing James received was a punctured lung. He couldn't even look me in my face during the trial. After deliberations were over, my attorney informed me that I was found not guilty. After I was released, I went straight home to my baby.

I had yet another fight on my hands because James wanted full custody of her. He had the nerve to think that I was going to let him take her from me without a fight. I was thinking to myself, he's a joke. He just hasn't had enough of torturing me.

I called him via phone and I asked him, "Do you really think I'm going to let you take my baby away from me? Are you serious?"

"I'll see you in court," he said.

I was devastated and replied, "Yes, you will see me with my lawyer present."

James never had a legal job and didn't have stability and the years of cocaine addiction fried his brain. The day of our custody hearing he informed Judge Toler I punctured his lung and he didn't think I was a fit mother. Dealing with his mess for as long as I did, I was prepared for the games he threw in my way. I showed the judge pictures of crack around the home, old restraining orders, and his criminal history as evidence. It only took the judge about forty-five minutes to deliberate. She ordered him to a random drug test, and he was only allowed supervised visits on the weekend. I was ecstatic, and it felt like a huge burden was taken off my shoulders.

Eventually, my baby and I got our own place. It was a struggle because I was a single mother and had to uphold all responsibilities on my own. I had to make adjustments with my work life so that my baby could get to and from daycare. Not only was I working, but also I was in the process of going back to school. I always asked myself, would life be different if I had listened to my parents? The reason for my legal trouble was thinking with my heart instead of my mind. The experience taught me an invaluable lesson about life. It made me a stronger and wiser woman. It influenced me to be a better mother and never put my baby in a situation that could cause her to be without me. I discovered that I didn't need a man or material things to validate me. Loving James wasn't healthy and wasn't good for me. Winning the trials made me look at life in a different perspective. My primary focus is my daughter's needs and welfare. The worse mistake of my life resulted in me losing freedom, job, house, and sanity. Words couldn't express the pain and heaviness of my broken heart. The whole idea of going from sugar to salt destroyed me. Every day I regret I didn't listen to my parents about staying in school. They knew what was best for me all along. As the wise woman, I learned that those who honor their parents' wishes in life could never go wrong.

Growing Up with Autism

Joshua Arnold

INTRODUCTION

When I was growing up, I didn't really know that I had autism. I only remember feeling weird and out of place, as if I was on another planet. It wasn't until I was 13 years old that I found out I had this seemingly wonderful psychological condition considered by many to be a mental disorder. I never looked at my autism as being a bad thing. In fact, later in life, I looked at it as more of an advantage than a disadvantage, especially when it came to my artwork. My story goes back to the period from 1992 to 2003 because this is the period when I didn't really know I had autism.

EARLY LIFE

I was born in Detroit, Michigan on September 7, 1990, to my mother, Karen, who had me at the hospital all by herself. I never had a dad in my life. He left before I was even born. As a child, I never even thought about the fact that I didn't have a dad, and whenever I asked my mother who my dad is or who my dad was, she said, "Yo Daddy is Jesus," or something along those lines. I thought to myself, "Yeah right!" I just laughed it off in a non-serious way.

Later on, I found out that he worked for General Motors, as part of a concept and design team, but I'll explain that later in the story so let's get back to the beginning.

The oldest memories I have are from when I was around two or three years old. The first house I ever lived in was an old white and grey colored house. It looked as if it were built in the 1960s or 1970s. It had a roof made of lightly colored green tiles. There were no fences around our house or even the houses next door. The neighborhood we lived in was somewhat between a suburban-like neighborhood and a ghetto. Some of the houses were well maintained while others were in disarray and looked as if they had been ransacked and abandoned.

I used to play on a swing day in and day out. That old swing was set on the side of the house near the backyard. It was black, aluminum colored, and it was covered with small rust spots. It had been there for some time. While swinging, I used to look up towards the tree line behind the houses across the street from our house and wonder what was beyond that point. Even at that time, I didn't really feel like I could grasp the reality of my situation. I only remember feeling strange and out of place as if my mind was in a different dimension than my body.

When I was two years old, I accidentally shocked myself by pouring water on a teddy bear lamp that my mother had on a small circular table, which stood in the corner of the living room. After I got shocked, I laughed instead of crying. That was the first time in my life that I took pain without crying. I guess that was my first unofficial autistic experience. I really didn't feel any pain; only an ecstatic hyperactive feeling. It felt like a burst of adrenaline had rushed through my body and then quickly wore off the second I let go of the lamp. Now that I look back on that day, I think that was the first autistic thing I've ever done in my life.

I was only three years old when my baby sister Josephine died. That day I was playing outside riding around on the side of the house on my big-wheel tricycle. All of a sudden, an ambulance had pulled up in front of our house and out came two paramedic people rushing towards our front door. One of paramedics was carrying a small stretcher-like device, and the other was carrying a large water-cooler-like box with a paramedic logo on it. They rushed into house but they came out shortly after only about nine or ten minutes. I never actually saw them take her body out of the house. I only saw them put the large water-cooler-like box into the back of the ambulance. Seconds later my mother came out and talked to them for about five minutes, but eventually they slowly began to pull off, and my mother just stood there watching and saying repeatedly as the ambulance slowly disappeared over the street horizon, "Oh lord! Oh lord! Oh lord, my baby!"

I didn't really understand the situation until a few years later. I was like six or seven years old when I heard my mother and grandmother talking about the events of that day. I don't really have many memories of my younger sister. In fact, I barely remember her at all. The only real memory I have of her was when I saw her sitting in her car seat laughing and making baby noises as she rocked back and forth. That was only a month before she died. She only lived to be three or four years old.

I can still remember the days of the year 1995 as I remember the back of my hand. I used to attend a kindergarten school. It was about two blocks from my house. I use to walk there every day with my older brother and two older sisters. We didn't have a car, and school buses didn't run though that area because it was kind of a bad neighborhood. My kindergarten teacher was a big hefty old lady who wore a brown wig and big coke-bottle glasses. I still can't remember her name, but I do remember her being an old-fashioned, happy-go-lucky person who always fell asleep by the end of the day. She eventually had to have an assistant come and take her place during the last three hours of the day. I was in kindergarten when I realized I had a speech impediment. Whenever I asked my teacher a question, it seemed as if I was talking too fast and no one could understand me. I had no problems fitting in with the rest of the kids. In fact, that was probably the only time before middle school that I really didn't have to try to fit in. Later on, when I was five or six years old, I found out I had asthma. As a little kid, I didn't realize I had autism because I had only attended kindergarten and first grade. At these levels, I fit in just as everyone else did because we were all learning at the same level and no one, not even my teachers, could tell at that grade level that I had special needs.

When I started first grade in 1997, I had two teachers. One was named Ms. Martin. She was a medium-sized, dark brown-skinned lady who always wore some kind of braided hair style. The other was named Ms. Barker who was also my main teacher in the second grade. She was a forty to fifty years old. She was an abusive old person. She was always ready to hit one of the students with a yardstick or ruler for even the slightest mistake or backtalk. She would say things like, "Back in my day we used to get our asses beat with a wooden paddle." I used to think she was the most annoying teacher ever. She was always trying her hardest to find a reason to beat one of us with her twelve-inch steel ruler, even for the littlest of things like talking too loudly or not finishing an assignment on time. Once she beat a girl for peeing on herself. That made the poor girl pee on herself a second time.

It was during my first and second grade years that I felt like I was out of place. I stayed up late at night even though

134

I knew I had to be at school the next day. While at school, I began to feel a little off balance. Whenever I would walk down long hallways, I would feel as if I was going to trip over myself. Maybe that was the autism kicking in. At that time, I did not know what was going on. All I knew was that school and schoolwork were starting to become a strenuous task to me. It felt as if I had to force myself to focus on even the most basic of first grade assignments. For example, I failed most of my math tests except the ones that dealt with addition or subtraction because I couldn't finish an assignment on time and I kept getting distracted by even the simplest of things like drawing on the desk or staring outside of the window. Back then, when the time ran out, the teachers did not just allow me to continue finishing my work. They would take my paper exactly when the timer stopped, and there was nothing I could do or say about it. When the teacher looked at my unfinished paper, she said, "Mr. Arnold! You had all the time you needed to finish this assignment. Why haven't you finished it?" I would just look at her and say, "I . . . I don't know . . . Ms. Martin. I guess I couldn't focus." What I said did not matter to her because she was one of those old-school teachers who would not take pity on any of her students unless they had a good reason, and to her I clearly did not have one.

Later that year I found out that I might have ADD or Attention Deficit Disorder. ADD and autism did not mix so well. First, it was already hard enough to focus when I did not fit in with the rest of the students in class. Second, most people with ADD tend to stare and glance at other people without realizing it half of the time, and that's exactly what happened to me.

One time I kept finding myself staring at a girl in my class named Eve. Eve was a light-skinned girl with light sandy brown hair and blue eyes. Like me, she was one of the taller kids in our class, along with about five other students. For some reason, I could not gather myself. Eve eventually noticed me randomly staring at her on multiple occasions until one day she gave me a shocked and disturbed look as if she were thinking, "What the f— are you looking at?" She then proceeded to move her desk to the back of the classroom next to a friend of hers, and I just sat there calmly thinking to myself, "Curse this brain of mine." For the remainder of that year Eve continued to ignore me, even when I did attempt to talk to her. I guess I could blame this incident on autism, but this was before I was diagnosed with it.

It was not until the third grade that I really began to notice that my mind was much different from the average person in my class. That was the year I started to feel like an outcast in a school I had attended for two years. The first time that I had my first real autistic experience was when I woke up one day and started watching one of my favorite anime television shows called Dragon Ball Z as I normally did before going to school. I was excited about the episode I had just watched and I couldn't wait to tell my friends about it.

When I got to school, I started walking to my first hour class. As I was walking, I started to think about what Mr. Libald had said the day before about our next assignment. At the same time, my thoughts on the Dragon Ball Z TV show were still going through my mind. Then, all of a sudden, the random sound of a loud vacuum cleaner started playing in the back of my mind. For a moment, I felt as if I could no longer control the thoughts that were going through my head. When I got to class, I felt as if my mind was in a whole other dimension. I walked into the classroom, took a seat, started staring at the chalkboard, and then I began to read the assignment written on the board while at the same time trying to drown out my thoughts by thinking of a song I had heard on a commercial the day before. My strategy began to work slowly but surely. I started to regain control over my own thoughts.

After that situation was over, I began to feel nervous and paranoid. I started wondering what that was. Clutching my pencil in my right hand, I quickly rubbed it off and said to myself, "Forget about it. It probably won't happen again." I took a deep breath and began writing down the assignment written on the board. Since that day, I felt like my mind had changed completely. Whether it was for the good or for the bad, I did not know.

INCESSANT TESTS AND QUESTIONS

By the time I was halfway done with third grade and started preparing myself for the fourth grade, my counselor at the school I was attending, Erma El Henderson, had started to think that something was wrong with me, and slowly I began to notice their attempts to figure out what was wrong with me.

Every two or three weeks, one of the school counselors would call out my name of the schools PA loudspeaker, "Joshua Arnold! Joshua Arnold! You need to report to the counselors' office ASAP." I got so embarrassed because kids who were called to the counselors' office were only the special-needs students, and most of my classmates loved to taunt and pick on anyone presumed "special!" I had to prepare myself for that later on, but now it was time for me to be questioned by the counselors.

About four or five different counselors questioned me. I cannot remember their names. I only remember the questions they asked me. At first, I tried to ignore the school counselors' advances by not answering most of their questions. That was until a female counselor asked me if I liked to draw. As an artist, I could not say no.

"Yeah. I like to draw. I like to draw ships and airplanes," I said with an ecstatic look on my face.

"Draw me a man with a phone in his hand," she said as she handed me a piece of paper and a pencil. I took the paper and pencil and slowly began to draw. As I was drawing, I could not help but look up at her face. However, for some reason I could not look her in the eyes without getting this strange vibrating like feeling in the back of my eyeballs. I could see she noticed that and wrote something down in her logbook. I saw this, but thought nothing of it and finished the drawing and gave it to her. She looked very pleased, but she did not say anything. The school bell rang, and I asked her if I could leave.

"Yes, of course. You can leave at any time," she said. I gave her a glaring look and I nervously proceeded back to my classroom as if nothing happened.

After returning to class, I sat down at my desk and started reading the assignment written on the chalkboard. As I looked out of the corner of my eyes, I could see at least three or four of my classmates giving me a strange look. I remember only one of those classmates by name. His name was Edward. Edward was a hyperactive kid who always liked talking shit and spreading rumors about people behind their backs. For the next couple of days, some of my classmates would ask me with a smirk look on their faces, "Hey, Josh, are you going to see your counselor friends again?" Trying to avoid having any arguments or discussions about that situation, I just ignored them.

In the meantime, I tried to focus on school activities. Luckily, my third grade teacher Mr. Liebald gave us some interesting homework assignments. One of them was researching mythical creatures like the Loch Ness monster and I could tell that he knew it would interest me. After class he asked me, "Hey! Mr. Arnold, did you know that the Loch Ness monster is supposed to be an ancient species of dinosaur called a plesiosaur?"

"No. I thought it was a sea serpent or something," I replied in astonishment.

He smiled at me, handed me the assignment sheet, and then retreated into the classroom. I walked home excited and repeatedly glancing at the assignment with a joyous look on my face. Sometimes I think Mr. Liebald knew I had autism. I think he also knew that I would get seriously interested in that type of homework assignment, which I did. I spent hours at the school library reading and looking up books related to the topic. I even started watching documentaries on the Loch Ness monster on TV at times when I would normally be watching cartoons or anime. I even started to draw concept sketches of what I thought the creature looked like, but this was not to last too long.

Eventually the school counselors started checking up on me again, asking me more questions. He would say, "Mr. Arnold, how do feel when you are talking to other students in your class?" or "Do you look your classmates in the eyes when you are talking to them?" Still trying to find out what was different about me. To me, there was nothing wrong with me other than a handful of situations where I felt out of place or had trouble controlling my basic senses. Other than that, I felt normal, but the school thought otherwise.

Throughout my third and fourth grade years, my counselors keep coming to my classroom just to send me to have an evaluation by some random instructor. This time, it was an older guy who looked about forty or fifty years of age. He would ask me many questions about my daily activities, who my friends were, what did I watch on TV, and what types of video games did I play, and list went on. Eventually, I felt as if most of those questions were for obedient or brainwashed kids who had already been trained to answer those questions. I also felt as if they were trying to compare me to other more standardized students as if I were inferior to whomever they considered "normal." It was at that time that I started to feel almost like an alien on a foreign planet. Therefore, I asked the counselor, "Can I go back to my classroom now?" To my surprise he said, "Sure . . . you can leave at any time." When he said that, I just left as if nothing happened.

MIDDLE SCHOOL YEARS

By the end of the fourth grade, the school had eventually decided to place me into a Special Education program until they could determine what was wrong with me.

In September 2000, I had been transferred to Parkman Middle School. I was now ten or eleven years old in the fifth grade, and by then my autism was making me emotionally unstable. I would find myself feeling a little depressed for no reason. I felt like I was trapped in a never-ending paranoid state of mind, worrying about nothing.

My fifth grade teacher was named Mr. Brian who was also a college professor. He was a tall, skinny guy with glasses. He seemed like he didn't really want to be there, and I couldn't really blame him. He seemed like he was having trouble trying to teach a special needs class, while at the same time having to teach college students on the weekends.

Each one of my fifth grade classmates had a different level of learning, or a different set of learning skills. Some had real learning disabilities like dyslexia or ADHD, while the rest of the class, like me, had been sent there because the Detroit Public School system could not determine what was wrong with us. Therefore, they just tossed us to Special Ed.

One of the people I made friends with in this class was a kid named Lamont. He was a tall kid who looked like Kevin Hart but with a semi-deep voice. At first, he seemed like a normal kid. He was well-mannered and he always finished his work on time. However, as the semester went along he began to punish himself whenever he felt he had done something wrong. While punishing himself he would mumble to himself, "I'm sorry! I won't mess up again . . ." He mumbled while he was slapping himself senselessly. Sometimes I tried to intervene by saying, "Lamont, what the hell are you doing? Slapping yourself isn't going to change the situation." But he would continue to do this to himself, especially when he thought that he was going to get suspended or kicked out of school. He wasn't the only student in the class who would act out in a strange way.

There was a girl in the class named Stevina. She was a short girl with long Jheri curl hair who always sat next to me and pretended as if she liked me or something. She would say things like, "Hey, Josh! How do I look today?" or "Josh what do you think about this dress that I have on?" and I would say something like, "Umm . . . you look great," or "I don't know. I am not really an expert on dresses. So you might have to ask someone else." I was just trying to play it off, but whenever I didn't respond the way she wanted, she attempted to get me in trouble by doing ridiculous things to herself and blaming it on me for no reason. One day she threw herself on the floor and pretended to cry while screaming for the teacher to come and help her, only to blame the whole incident on me. After a short while, I realized that this chick was crazy and she was just trying to attract attention to herself. After that ordeal, I began to sit next to a kid named Corey. That wasn't his real name. I just called him that because I could not remember his real name so I just nicknamed him Corey. He would call me "Joshu" because he spoke with an accent and couldn't pronounce the 'A' sound at the end of my name. Corey was a Chinese foreign exchange student from Manchuria. I could tell that he hadn't really been in the U.S. that long. He was still trying to get used to pronouncing some of the basic English words like cup, hat, shoe, and dictionary. I would burst out laughing whenever he would yell, "Shu! Shu!" struggling to pronounce the word shoe, but he was still one of my best friends throughout my fifth grade year.

While in fifth grade Special Ed, I found that our class assignments were simplified so that all of the students would be on the same level. As I said before, everyone in the class had a different level of reading and writing skills. Some were on a fifth grade level, while others were only on the level of a kindergartener. I didn't really notice this until I began reading over our first class assignment and I just sat there thinking to myself, "This crap is too easy!" Our first class assignment looked as if it were made for someone who was just getting ready to enter the first grade. I had to do ABC's, counting shapes, and even addition all over again.

After about two months of easy homework and classroom assignments, even our teacher, Mr. Brian, began to notice how quickly half the class would finish their assignments. One day, while grading papers, he asked me, "Why are you in this class, Mr. Arnold? You don't look as if you are having any trouble understanding any of these assignments."

"I really don't know. I was placed in this class by the DPS department. These class assignments are the same kind of assignments that I had when I was in the first or second grade," I replied.

And he simply said, "Oh . . ." in calm voice as he smiled and continued to grade our assignments. When I look back on this, I sometimes think that he knew how broken the DPS school board was at that time especially when it came to kids who were labeled as mentally challenged or mentally unfit, but he probably just didn't say anything about it, at least not to us anyway.

When my fifth grade year finally came to an end I was transferred to another school called Munger Middle School, which was in my old neighborhood. In order to attend this school I had to go and live with my grandmother for a year until my mother and I could refurbish the house next door. This was also the same neighborhood that I grew up in from the time I was a baby up until kindergarten. By now, most of the kids I went to kindergarten with had long gone, and I needed to make new friends at home and eventually at my new school when the school year started.

The first person I made friends with in my old neighborhood was a kid named Dietrich. He was a short, skinny kid with a big head. Like me, he was considered an outcast to most of the young people in the neighborhood. Sometimes the kids in the neighborhood would call him "Starvin Marvin" after a cartoon character from a TV show called *South Park*. He responded by yelling, "Nigga! Shut yo gremlin-looking ass up." I burst out laughing every time he said that. I'm glad he never took anything they said seriously.

Dietrich did not have autism. He was only socially awkward because of his family who kind of disowned him and his mother because she was a lesbian and his family was religiously conservative. This eventually led to him and his mother moving from neighborhood to neighborhood. Because of this continuous moving around, Dietrich did not develop enough socially because he was not able to make friends in the short amount of time that they lived in each neighborhood. Situations like this were among the reasons why I disliked religion as a kid. I could not for life of me get why religious families picked their invisible deities over their physical family members. Now that I think about it, I don't think I was ever really a religious person. Even as a child, I thought most of the religions that I came across to be interesting at first, but the more I read into them the more I started to see why many people from these religions can never really get along with people from other religious groups or religious backgrounds.

For example, as a kid I saw Christians in my neighborhood and on TV hating, bashing, or being paranoid about other religious groups like Muslims, Hindus, and Buddhists. I would hear them constantly making up all kinds of paranoid and delusional ideas about these groups and even teaching their children to dislike these religious groups. I also saw these same situations happening in other religious cultures. For example, in the Muslim world there are feuds between the two main groups: the Sunnis and Shiites. The same thing happens in Hinduism and Buddhism as well. For example, there was a civil conflict in Myanmar in which Buddhist and Muslim civilians were being brainwashed by their spiritual leaders to confront one another. Situations like these convinced me to believe that most religions are just cults for adults and that most parents drag their children into this mess by being brainwashed at a young age to continue the crap that their parents were involved in when these parents were growing up.

THE FATHER WHO NEVER WAS . . .

Dietrich and I always played Pokémon cards with each other for days on end before school officially started in September of the year 2001, which was also my sixth grade year, and the same year I would meet my dad for the first time. I first ran into my dad when my mother, my grandmother, and I were leaving out of the side entrance of a Home Depot store and all of a sudden my mother yelled, "Well look who's over there . . . Hey James! Heeeeey! It's me Karen! Come and see your son!" My dad was loading some hardware onto the back of his truck, and then he slowly walked towards us while we were walking mildly fast towards him. When we finally stopped I just stood there staring at him. To me, he looked somewhat strange. He was a light-skinned guy who almost looked Caucasian. He was wearing a white T-shirt with blue jean shorts, some Nike sneakers, and an old-fashioned sunhat, which I thought was kind of goofy-looking especially for someone who was forty-seven or forty-eight years old.

I looked up at his face trying to see his eyes, but his sunglasses covered his eyes and he had a strange grin-like smile on his face. Then all of a sudden, in medium-tone voice he said, "Hey kid!" I was too nervous to reply, so I just smiled and waved my hand back at him.

My mother and grandmother walked over to him and began to have a short conversation. Two or three feet behind them, I just stood there listening to my mother, my grandmother, and my dad talk about the good old days, the days way before I was born. I wasn't really paying any attention to what they were saying. I just stood there looking and watching them talk to one another and watching their facial expressions while I was also thinking to myself, "They seem to get along

145

well. I wonder why my mom and dad didn't stay together!" In the back my mind I wanted to ask them that question while they were standing there talking, but my mind got the best of me and just zoned out. My parents and my grandmother continued their conversation for about three or four minutes before we departed from the Home Depot.

The next day my mother and I left the home early in the morning. She said we were going to get something to eat.

"Why didn't we just eat breakfast at home?" I asked.

"Boy! Did you forget that today is your birthday?" she said.

I had totally forgotten about September the seventh. A few minutes later, we stopped at a McDonald's, and guess who was there? My dad, wearing a similar getup to the outfit he had on the previous night, except this time he was wearing sandals instead of gym shoes. He looked as if he knew I would be coming to meet him at this particular McDonald's. We sat down at his table, and he and my mother began to talk about their everyday lives. I switched my seat, moved over to a table across from them, and got distracted by thoughts running though my own mind. Half an hour later, my dad got up and said, "I'm about to leave." Before he left, he gave me a 100 dollar bill and said, "Happy Birthday, son!" as he got up from his seat and walked out of the restaurant. He got into his red 1997 Ford-F-150 pickup truck and left the McDonald's as quickly as he had come. That was the last time I ever saw my dad. Later on that day, my mother told me that he lived in Texas.

"Texas!" I said in a loud and ecstatic voice.

"Yeah!" she said, and that was it. After that day I felt kind of relieved, as if that chapter in my life was finally solved even though it really wasn't, at least not completely.

AUTISTIC PERSPECTIVE ON 9/11

School started a few days later. The first day of my sixth grade year did not start well. That morning I accidentally overslept and got to my first class late. My new teacher, whose name I did not even know then nor can I remember it now, began arguing with me over what time all students were supposed to be in class. Also that was September, 11, 2001, and the 9/11 event was reported live on TV while we were doing our first class assignment. While watching the events on TV, most of the class, including the teacher, was in shock and awe shouting things like, "Oh shit! Look at that. That shit looks crazy as hell!" and "Man, that's some f—ed up shit right there." I just watched with dazed facial expression as if I had already seen this before. In fact, I have seen similar scenes of destruction in war documentaries. As a kid, I always loved to watch military documentaries about wars, uprisings, natural disasters, and what we now call terrorist attacks. Therefore, this was nothing new to me. I had seen similar events while watching World War II and Cold War documentaries, and like most autistic people, I had no real empathy or emotions or even a reaction to that situation. It was like watching a bombing raid on a small town during WWII or an airstrike on a village in Vietnam, except on 9/11 only two or three buildings were destroyed instead of a dozen houses.

The remainder of my sixth was boring. For most of that year, I found myself being sent to classroom after classroom because the school could not find a permanent teacher to teach special education classes, and, man, was I happy when my sixth grade year finally came to an end in 2002.

AUTISTIC REVELATIONS

In late 2003, when I was 13 years old, I finally found out that I had autism. One afternoon, the Detroit Board of Education phoned my mother and informed her that they had sent copies of my school and medical records to a special child psychologist in order to be evaluated. The evaluator would figure out what type of disability I had. One day my mother and I went to go see this child psychologist in order to figure out what school administrators and counselors had failed to figure out during all these years, and that day was to be one of the strangest days of my life in what it revealed.

We drove to a child psychiatric center located in downtown Detroit. I can't remember the name of this place, but I do remember the three-story gray brickwork building with black and white stripes going down its side. When we stopped to get out of the car, I asked my mother, "Ma, what do you think the psychologist will say?"

"I don't know," she replied in a sarcastic tone of voice.

When we went inside to see the psychologist, he opened the door to greet us.

"Hello, come in and have a seat over there," he said as he was pointing to some red and white chairs in front of his desk. The psychologist was a pudgy, fifty-seven year old man in a lab coat with an old-fashioned James Bond–like hairstyle that looked as if it dated to the 1980s. He also had a thin mustache. When we finally sat down, the psychologist asked me, "So Mr. Arnold, what brings you to my humble office?" He said that in a happy-go-lucky tone of voice.

"I came to have my disability evaluated based on the medical records the school sent you," I replied.

He then proceeded to pull out a large stack of documents and files from the drawer under his desk, and began to glance and scroll through them.

"Your last name is Arnold, right?" He asked and I immediately said "yeah" in a low tone of voice. He then proceeded to say in nonchalant tone of voice, "Okay, Mr. Arnold, based on your medical records and the reports from your school and the records sent by your counselors, I have concluded that you, in fact, have Asperger's Syndrome."

"Ass Burgers Syndrome! What's that?" I asked.

Not even my mother had heard of this diagnosis before.

"Do you think that Agent Orange could somehow be responsible for my son's Asperger's Syndrome?"

My mother's question changed my whole perspective of my situation.

"I don't know. I've never heard of any connection between Agent Orange and autism, but it's possible."

"I asked you this because my son's father has Agent Orange, and he got it during the war, the Vietnam War," my mother said to the psychologist. I just sat there stunned. All this time I never knew that my dad had fought in the Vietnam War or that he had Agent Orange. It made perfect sense. I had finally pieced it all together in the back of my mind. My dad might have left me because of psychological issues he might have developed during the war. He probably was like so many other war veterans I had seen up until that point.

What made the situation even weirder for me was the idea that my Asperger's might have been a direct result of chemical warfare in a conflict that I had nothing to do with. In a way, you could say that was a good thing because I saw the full series of the events that lead to me being born with Asperger's Syndrome.

In Search of Love

CHRISTINE MAJOR

I am Christine Michelle Price and I was brought into this world at Providence Hospital in Southfield, Michigan on September 21, 1974. My mother, Patricia, was nineteen years old when she gave birth to me. My birth certificate states, "Father: Unknown." I wonder if my father was even there to witness my birth, the birth of his little baby girl. Growing up without a father, no pictures, and no memories of him was very difficult for me. Here is my story. I will tell it to you unadulterated and as I remember it without changes or cosmetics.

BEGINNINGS

At the tender age of three or four, I recall memories of living with my grandmother and my Bumpa on 18255 Kentfield, Detroit at Evergreen and McNichols. Grandpa was not an easy word for me, therefore Bumpa stuck. I know I was the apple of his eye. I truly loved my Bumpa. I have only a couple of photos of him and I miss him very much. While at his work in a factory in 1978, my Bumpa passed away due to a heart attack at the age of sixty-four.

Grandmother had six children with my Bumpa, four boys and two girls: Uncle Richard, Aunt Margaret, Mother, Uncle Michael, Uncle Gary, and lastly, Uncle Daniel. Uncle Richard was drafted to Vietnam and was killed there in 1968. Aunt Margaret got married and had two children: Dennis

151

and Katie. She worked on the transmission assembly line at General Motors. Uncle Michael never married, never had children, and never moved from Grandmother's home. Uncle Gary was disabled. He could not read, write, or speak. As an adult, he resided in assisted living homes. My uncle Daniel was my favorite when I was a child. He played Atari with me, and we had pillow fights. He acknowledged me a lot.

Mother was close with her sister Margaret who lived on Ashton Street between Constance and Joy in Detroit. Therefore, we went there and visited often. My cousins, Dennis and Katie, and I cuddled on the couch with our cozy blankets. We watched *He-Man and the Masters of the Universe*. When outside playing, we rode our big wheels up and down the street and made mud pies in the driveway by the side door.

ABUSIVE ENVIRONMENT

Since Bumpa passed in 1978, we started spending more time at Aunt Margaret's place. Aunt Margaret and Mother were working together to find a place that we could call home. We found one in Mansfield, Detroit. It was a mile south of Aunt Margaret's. It was a Warrendale Community home for just Mom and me. We didn't have a lot of money, but Grandmother helped out, and Mother had Government aid to help out. Mother and I grew close together in our new home. Uncle Daniel would come over to visit, and we would have McDonald's Quarter Pounder eating competitions. I was always the winner. When Aunt Margaret and the family came to visit us, we all went to White Castle to eat.

Just before kindergarten, Mother had a boyfriend for a short time, maybe three years. His name was Mel Roach. He was very arrogant, controlling, and jealous. My bedroom was just above Mother's. I was in my room one evening and I overheard an argument between them. He was yelling about how we did not need charity from a neighbor that helped our family when we were in need by bringing milk and bread. I was hurt by the way he treated my mother. Soon after that they went their separate ways, and Mel moved out.

I started kindergarten in the fall of 1980. My school was on the South side of West Warren, and we lived on the North side. I was scared but excited about my first day of school. Mother walked me to and from school every day across the busy road. My teacher was a Spanish woman with medium-length, dark hair. I enjoyed her. She taught us to sing songs and say numbers in Spanish. Our kindergarten room was separated from the other classrooms. We were across from the school office and next to the entry doors. Kindergarten was only half days, and we did not have much interaction with the children in the higher grades.

First grade and second grade were okay in the beginning. In third grade things changed at school. I was being bullied, pushed around, and called names. One afternoon in school, I was pushed down a flight of steps and had a chunk of asphalt thrown in my eye while I was on the playground. I walked home crying. This was my mother's breaking point. She called Grandmother, and together they made a decision to send me to St. Christopher Catholic School. This school was on our side of West Warren, and it was four streets from ours. I walked to and from school every day. Going to a new school, starting the fourth grade, and wearing a required uniform daily were all quite different than I was used to. I was terrified about what to expect. I struggled to belong again. This transition did not go well. With my last name as Price, everyone made fun of me.

153

They called me Fisher-Price, the Price is Right, and asked how much did I cost. This made me feel alone, hurt, worthless, and self-loathing. I made only one friend, Danielle, in the fourth grade and I struggled academically. Therefore, I was held back to repeat the fourth grade, and my one and only friend went on to the fifth grade.

My uncle Daniel lived with us during this time after his first divorce from Lynda. He had no children. He had a couple of girlfriends, Ralphie and Carrie.

Holiday visits at Grandmother's house started becoming unpleasant since Bumpa passed away six years ago. Uncle Michael was drinking and getting drunk and obnoxious, and everyone left. He became alcoholic and eventually he started using crack cocaine. He also became verbally and physically abusive to my Grandmother and he took her money to satisfy his drug habit. In addition, he would come to our home while I was in school and become verbally and physically abusive to my mother. He dragged her around by her long, beautiful brown hair, shouted profanities, and took money from her if she had any. I went home from school on many occasions when these incidents had taken place to find Mother in a corner of the living room or bedroom crying and sometimes bruised. I began to have hatred toward what my Uncle Michael had become. I was too young to stop it and I didn't know what to do. He was angry and bitter and he rarely showed love.

FINDING A FATHER AND A BROTHER

Mother got into a relationship with Aunt Margaret's brother in law, Danny, a divorced father of one son he did not see. Danny drove semi-truck over the road for a living. This required him to be gone sometimes six months at a time. He moved in with Mother and me, and soon I called him "Dad." Uncle Daniel moved out and in with Lori and her little boy, Jimmy, from her first marriage.

March 2, 1987, Mother gave birth to my half-brother, Jason Aaron Petrie. I was thirteen and full of excitement that I finally had a baby brother to love after being an only child for so many years. Our family seemed complete: Dad, Mom, Jason, and I. In my sixth and seventh grade years I was still being teased, bullied, and called names at St. Christopher School.

Mother worked at Hudson's Distribution Center. It was a good-paying job with benefits. Mother worked the morning shift while I was in school. Our neighbor, Connie, babysat my little brother until I got home from school. Under the surface, Mother and Father were having issues. One of these issues was his long over-the-road trips. These absences were hard on family life. The other issue was his infidelities. Father had been unfaithful to Mother and strayed from the marriage on two known occasions. Mother was doing all she could to keep it all together when, in fact, everything was slowly spiraling out of control.

FINDING A SOUL MATE

In the winter of 1988, I met my soul mate, Mike. I was working after school at Primo's Pizza on West Warren afternoons until eleven as a dishwasher. Mike was a newcomer from Georgia, and he stayed with his sister, Gail, who worked at the Ford Wayne assembly plant as an auto painter. Mike worked for food for his brother, Ted, who was on the payroll, and for the owner John at the Clock restaurant directly next door to the

Primo's Pizza. A short time later, he was hired at the restaurant and he would come to Primo's for pizza. He did not go to my school, nor was he in school. In fact, he was fifteen years older than I was. When I met him, I was still living at home, going to school, watching my brother, and working. Mike started taking me back and forth to school. I was still struggling academically through my eighth grade year and I was still being degraded. With Mike coming in the picture, I was labeled a whore for having a boyfriend fifteen years older than me. Again, I was to be held back to repeat the eighth grade. I did not repeat eighth grade at all.

LOSING THE MAN I CALLED FATHER

Father did not approve of my relationship with Mike. Because he was not my biological father, he could not do anything about it. Mom and Dad sent me away to stay with a family friend thinking this would change things, but it did not. In fact, I came back to my mother's home. Mother and Father split up when Jason was one-and-a-half years old. When I finally felt like I had a father, he was gone.

LOSING MY MOTHER

Mother packed up herself, Jason, and me. We left our home on Mansfield and moved in with my uncle Daniel, his then current wife, Lori, and her little son, Jimmy, from her first marriage. We lived in Westland on Birchwood near Wayne Road and Cherry Hill. This became home. Mother thought all this would lead to a better life. For a little while, everything seemed to be okay. Mike came to pick me up. Every chance we had to spend together, we did. I was trying to attend Marshal Public School around the corner from my uncle Daniel's home to repeat my eighth grade year. Meanwhile, Mother met John, and he himself had a son and was in and out of his relationship with Carrie, the mother of his child. I did not personally care for John because I did not like the way he treated my mother by going back and forth between the two women.

Mom had dealt with so much, she finally shut down. She would not come out of her room and she did not go to work. She became isolated and depressed. She had given up and shut us all out. I was losing my connection with my mother. I was confused, and everything was falling apart at the speed of light for me. Mother finally had a breakdown. She called Danny and told him to pick up Jason and his stuff. She couldn't take it anymore. Jason was two years old when Father came to pick him up with all his stuff. Dad and his then new female companion, Laurie Beth, raised Jason. I never really had any contact with Jason after we were separated except attending a couple of his birthday parties.

Laurie Beth was one of Father's infidelities. They hooked up, and he moved in with her during the divorce with Mother. I had lost my only baby brother. I did not get to see him grow up. Laurie Beth did not care too much for me because I was not a biological child of Danny. Because Laurie Beth did not feel I was family, I slipped through the cracks somewhere along the line of conception, and I felt that I was robbed of a Father.

Lori eventually reached her breaking point with my mother and called from work and told Mother she had to move out, that she was not contributing at all. I was helping her with all I could from babysitting Jimmy to house cleaning. We never saw Mother except to eat and use the bathroom. Mother moved out and left most of her stuff in Lori's garage. Most of the stuff went to the curb when she never returned for it. Mother went to stay with Grandmother for a short time before she moved in with John in Westland.

WHEN DOES THIS END?

The summer of 1989, Mike picked up all my belongings from Lori, and I moved in with him in an apartment in Detroit. Before I moved in with Mike, he seemed a bit controlling. Being young and naïve, I did not have a clue. Shortly after moving in with Mike, about six months into our relationship, he became more controlling and violent. I dealt with verbal, mental, and physical abuse from him for a period of five years. I never went back to school and never got the chance to complete my eighth grade year.

Soon after I moved in with Mike, I had become pregnant, and one month before my sixteenth birthday on August 20, 1990, I delivered a beautiful baby girl. She was seven pounds and six ounces, and we called her Nicole Marie Major. I became scared and obedient to my child's father. Mike, before leaving for work on several occasions, became angry. He went through, broke things, dumped out kitchen drawers on the kitchen floor, and left me to clean the mess. Hopeless and helpless, I thought this would be my life. Suzie, most of the time, came up and helped me clean my apartment and the messes that he left, and she let me cry on her shoulder. I met Suzie through a childhood friend of Mike, John Head. Suzie and John moved into the apartment down below ours.

WHEN THINGS SEEM TO GET BETTER . . .

Mike, now a painter, got a job through his brother, Tom. They painted low-income housing, and John was Mike's right hand man. The boss of the painting company passed all the sites and jobs to Mike because he was going through a divorce. We owned "Major Painting" company and we bought the four-unit apartment building we were living in. We rented out three of the units and continued living in the fourth. John and Sue moved into one of the apartments, as did another childhood friend of Mike's, Robert Toben, and his wife and two little boys. My mother lived in one of the apartments at one time.

Mike and I moved out and bought a house in Detroit. My mother was renting another home we had purchased just down the street on the opposite side. This was an upper and lower duplex house, and Mother had the lower duplex. Our second daughter, Jessica Ann Major, was born on September 6, 1994, at eight pounds, eight ounces. Mike bought a building for us to run our painting company out of just up the street on West Warren and Minock. The girls were raised in an office when they were young.

When Jessica was six months old, Mike came home from work one evening in what I called 'rare form' and pursued an argument with me about unfinished laundry. The next thing I knew, we were having an all-out brawl, and he was throwing laundry all over the place. I was trying to stop him, but he got angry and physical. He kept on punching and beating me until my left side was completely bruised. He then forced me to leave without the children. Locked out of my home, I walked to the corner and used the payphone to call the police. I waited forty-five minutes for the police to arrive. Upon their arrival, the police arrested Mike and took him to jail. The State of

159

Michigan picked up Domestic Violence Charges against him, requiring him to complete anger management courses, probation, and pay fines. Meanwhile, he had a restraining order placed on him to stay away from the children and me. I felt lost, angry, unloved. I was wondering why was of this happening to me? After Mike completed all the requirements for the court, he made amends with me and returned home.

REACHING ROCK BOTTOM . . .

Again, we move to Dearborn Heights. In 1995 Nicole started Kindergarten at Bedford Elementary and went on to complete first and second grades. On October 19, 1996, Mike and I took our wedding vows. Nicole was six, and Jessica was two years old. Within three years after we married, I fell into a dark hole for what seemed like an eternity. Mike introduced me to cocaine. In the beginning, using cocaine was random, then it spiraled from holidays to weekends, to a couple of times each week, and then it ended up being a daily practice. I lost myself in this addiction. Days, months, and years began to pass in an instant, or so it seemed to me. First, I began using it for fun, then I used it to fill voids and to find missing pieces. In the beginning, it seemed to make all my troubles disappear. Then I realized I lost years of my life. I failed my girls as they lost their mother for seven years. I remember feeling as if I was losing control of my own life. I was being controlled by the devil of addiction that sucked me into an abyss. I remember walking Jessica to school on her first day of kindergarten while I was "high as a kite." I didn't have a clue what rock bottom was or what it meant, but I was there.

160

THE AWAKENING

My awakening, or so I thought, came in July 1999 when the police were called and I was arrested for possession of cocaine. I had Jessica with me, not even five years old yet. Mike was contacted to come and get Jessica. Though the baggies were empty, they ran a toxicology screen that came back positive for cocaine. I sat in jail for three days, alone and scared. This was still not rock bottom. I was released with a pending court date that I returned for. I barely made it through my probation because I was still getting "high." I amended all my faults, completed my probation, and my record was expunged. May 19, 2000, Mike purchased a home in Farmington Hills on a dirt road with a country-like setting. Mike moved the family, thinking it would change life for the better. I was using cocaine, and so was he, though he quit long before I did.

THE POWER OF WILL

The summer of 2003 I went on a camping trip with my Mom, her husband Bob, my brother Jason, Mike, Jessica, Nicole, and I. Earlier that morning I had taken a pregnancy test that came back positive! Was this God giving me another chance at motherhood? I continued to use crack cocaine until three months before giving birth to my son. A miracle baby, Michael Richard Major was born on February 12, 2004. He was a healthy, beautiful, and non-drug-addicted baby. My quit day was November 26, 2003. It was of my own free will. With will power, and with no inpatient treatment or rehabilitation, I never used drugs again. On September 15, 2006, our family was blessed again with another baby girl. Her name was Emily Clair Major. She made our family complete.

In 2007 I went to Oakland Community College and took a personal finance course, a business management course, and a first responder course and passed all of them with As. I had support from the girls. Mike was not much support. Most of the time I came home from school while he was sleeping and our two eldest girls were tending to their little brother and sister.

FALLING APART

Nicole graduated high school in 2008, and Aunt Sue came from Alabama for the graduation party we had. The Monday after the graduation party Mike was being mental and verbal which was what he's transitioned to. After taking his anger management he has not put one hand on me. As I was driving Aunt Sue to the airport that morning for her flight, I realized my marriage was falling apart and that it really wasn't a marriage at all.

My birthday came and went again. Mike was just becoming crude, rude, and disrespectful. In August 13, 2009, I began an affair with our computer technician, Dave. He made me feel like a normal woman. I hated that my own husband didn't even see me. I felt invisible to him and I tried to make him pay attention to me, but he did not. On September 26, 2009, I had reached my breaking point and filed for divorce. I wanted to feel like a normal woman. I wanted to feel desired for who I was. I did not think that was too much to ask. I wondered sometimes: if something happened to me, would Mike then see me?

October 2009, Nicole moved out to an apartment with her boyfriend, Danny. This made me a little hurt. I felt she left because her dad and I couldn't get along for even five minutes. The drama became too much for Nicole, and she started having anxiety. As time passed, I noticed that she became okay. I believe it was for the better.

I moved out of the wedlock house and took the kids to live with me in a one-bedroom apartment because the arguments with Mike were just out of control. These arguments were in no way constructive or healthy for him, the children, or me. I was still in a so-called relationship with Dave who also had a significant other, but he was not married to her. With Dave, I felt like a woman but I also felt guilty. I felt trapped and could see no other way to get Mike open his eyes and see his "family."

BACK TOGETHER

In February 2010, and after many conversations that made me feel comfortable enough that we could salvage what was left of our marriage, I went back to Mike and cancelled the divorce. Lest things fall apart again, I kept my apartment lease until June 2010. Things were okay, and slowly we were going back to what was normal for our family. Shortly after my return, verbal and mental abuse came back. We hit an iceberg in our marriage, and I had had enough.

Aunt Suzie and her husband, Rick, moved back to Michigan on Merrick in Dearborn.

In November 2011, I obtained my mother's address after telling family members I really needed her. She and I hadn't been on speaking terms for a couple of years. After receiving my mom's address, I packed up the children and moved in with my mother and her husband, Bob. Meanwhile, I contacted a better attorney and I filed for divorce again.

After staying with my mom for a month, I found a home in Dearborn Heights for the kids and me. We moved in and made ourselves at home: no drama, no yelling, and no arguments, just peace and quiet. Mike did everything he could to get to me, and I just kept telling him that he was putting his head in the sand because our marriage was done with. It was over. I had to make him understand I needed him to be the man he should have been a long time ago or there was no change. I took the kids to school in Farmington every day and let them finish out their year. Jessica was in her senior year, and that made life much harder because I had to worry about all her graduation and what all its requirements. Mike was not being nice about helping us financially or in any way for that matter. I held out until March 2012 when we went to the friend of the court and I then cancelled the divorce for a second time.

While he had been working on changing his behavior, I made it clear that I would accept nothing short of the respect our children and I deserved. I had made up my mind that if he wanted this family he had to work for it. He had done nothing but work at our marriage every day since I left him alone in Farmington. I knew there was a man inside him, but he needed to learn how to be a husband, a father, and a friend. He had to learn to love himself before he could love us. I did not and will not move back to Whitlock. I have stood my ground. I am happy here on Campbell, and the kids are happy too.

Mike and I are stronger in our marriage today than ever. In April 2012, he moved to live with the children and me on Campbell. We worked together daily taking the necessary steps to save our family. In September 2012, I signed up for

164

school at Everest as a Medical Assistant. While studying for my medical diploma, I achieved my General Adult Education Diploma Certificate, with their help. I did well and I passed with honors. In July 2013, I completed my externship for my Medical Assistant Diploma. I did not want to stop there in my life. I have higher expectations for my children and myself. Therefore, I have decided to keep reaching for the stars. I then set forth a plan to attend Henry Ford College. I am currently attending Henry Ford College in the General Studies to reach my main goal of becoming a BSN, Bachelors of Science in Nursing.

The indelible mark in my heart, of what I have done, I still carry today. I have a great relationship with all my children and my husband. I have made amends where I could and left the rest alone. This I would not wish on my worst enemy. And I would not change anything. These life experiences have made me who I am today. We have all learned the true meaning of family. Whether it was good, bad, or ugly, communication is key in relationships. Love is what makes our house a home. Trust is the foundation our family is built on. Most of all, patience is virtue. My kids and my husband have been my biggest fans, cheering me through school, and I know in my heart of hearts that I am supported, loved, and respected.

The Journey of My Life

Nishwone Mohsin

I was a small-town boy born in 1994 to a Caucasian American teenage mother who converted to Islam and a teenage father who is an American Yemeni Muslim. My grandfather was always very special to me. There is not a day that passes when he does not cross my mind. I am the oldest of nine children. I have six sisters and two brothers. Three of my sisters were adopted by my parents when I was ten years of age. Moving from a small town to a big city was a hard adjustment, but now when I look back on it I could never be that small-town boy again. I went on vacation to Yemen four times. The first time was with my uncle, and we stayed for one month.

I look up to the strongest, most optimistic, and compassionate woman in my life. This woman struggles with chronic pain every single day and seems to somehow have a smile on her face. This beautiful woman is my mother.

THE DAY MY DAD MET MY MOM

My parents fell in love at first sight even though they encountered some difficulties with the family because they came from different backgrounds. However, their love had no limits, and everything worked out. My mother's family started to come around and accept my father. They got married, and I was their first child. My mother started studying about Islam, and shortly after that she converted.

My father had immigrated to America in pursuit of a better life and to live the American dream. My mother told me the story of when my father had plans to go back eventually to Yemen and get married, but that all changed when he met my mother. My father is my role model. He inspires me to be the best I can be. We have a great relationship. He is loving and caring and is the rock that holds our family together. We do almost everything together, and he taught me to be the man I am today.

When I was a young boy, my father loved sports cars. He went through his share of sports cars. He went back and forth between Mustangs and Camaros for several years. He sold his last sports car when I was twelve years old. It must have been a phase because nowadays he drives a minivan. When I was around four years old, my father had started the Mustang to let it warm up. I snuck into the car without my parents seeing me and I locked all the doors. Outside the car my parents were in a panic trying to get me to unlock the door because the car was started. They were holding a dollar up to the window trying to bribe me to unlock the door, but it was not working.

I slid my little body down the seat and started to rev the gas pedal. It was a good thing it was a stick shift because if I would have tried to shift it, it would have stalled. My mother stood by the car window as my father walked toward our other vehicle acting as if he was going to leave. That was all it took me to get out. I yelled, "Daddy, Daddy, wait for me." I always loved to go with my father everywhere. I think that was the scariest thing I put my parents through.

THE MEMORIES OF MY LATE GRANDFATHER

He is gone but never forgotten. Time does ease pain. When I was not with my father, I was with my grandparents. Even though I was a Muslim child and Grandpa was a Christian, we had the strongest bond. He spoiled me since the day I was born. Most of my weekends were spent with him. We went bike riding, camping, and fishing. Every now and then we snuck off to McDonald's to get an ice cream cone when Grandma was not around. She did not like Grandpa to eat sweets because he was a diabetic. At the time, I was just happy to get an ice cream cone. I did not know that it could harm my Grandpa's health. Looking back, I understand now why my grandma did not like to see him eat sweets.

On April 2001, my Grandpa suffered from a stroke and ended up in the hospital and never returned home. My parents and I visited him about four times a week in the hospital. Just when we thought things were getting better, they got worse. His kidneys started to fail, and his body began to shut down and started to retain fluids. Eventually, he had to be put on a life support machine. At this point, he could not talk, but we always talked to him because in our hearts we felt that he could hear every word we were saying. I never knew what losing a loved one felt like until that fateful summer day of June 2, 2001, when my Grandpa passed away. I was a young boy. I did not quite understand death and why my Grandpa had to go. With the help of my loving parents, things started to seem normal after a while. I will always love Grandpa.

MY BIG FAMILY

I have three biological sisters, three adopted sisters, and two biological brothers. Being the oldest of nine children left no dull moment in my life. It is always hectic, but I would not change a thing in it. We are always there for each other and we are very protective of one another. We have learned how to compromise. We learned to be giving and to be compassionate.

It gets a little crazy in my crowded household: crying, screaming, he said, she said. Waiting on the bathroom for an hour and taking long road trips is always a challenge. At the end of the day our love for one another is what binds us together. I learned what is important in life. It is not the materialistic things; it is my family. In my large family the little things make us smile. Sitting together on the back porch telling jokes for hours at a time, barbeques, playing sports, and watching movies together are invaluable times. People may look at us strangely when seeing all of us in public together. If only they knew what a blessing it is in having a big family.

Mid-June 2004 was when my parents adopted my three sisters. My mother's sister was their biological mother. She had an addiction called alcoholism and she struggled with her addiction until this day. This caused her to lose her three daughters. The Child Protective Services (CPS) took them from her. Even though my parents already had five kids of their own at the time, they could not bear to see our cousins lost forever. For a few months, my parents were in and out of the courtroom fighting to get custody of my aunt's children. They were in foster care. My mom lost hope. They would remain in foster care, she thought. One morning, my mom received a surprising phone call from the CPS worker asking her if she still wanted her nieces. My parents were filled with joy, and they could not believe it. My parents believed in keeping a family together. Even though they knew that a bigger family would be challenging, they said, "It was worth the challenge."

In March of 2010, my mother had my youngest brother. That was when we became a family of eleven. The day when my parents came home with him, we all were waiting at the door to welcome his arrival. He is my precious little brother and he completes our family.

FACING DIFFICULTIES

I was born in Coldwater, Michigan, a very small town. At first, living in a small town was not all that bad. I had a lot of friends. Never once did I feel out of place until that day of 9/11. It was like everything changed. People started looking at us differently because of our religious beliefs. My family didn't even feel safe. We could not walk down the streets without being verbally attacked.

After 9/11, I noticed people started to change; I was very young and could not understand why. When my mom and I would walk down the street people yelled out remarks such as, "Go back to your own country, you sand nigger," and "Camel jockey, you do not belong here." It was very strange to hear that because I am an American. I was born and raised in America. Also my mother has never been to a foreign country in her life. We could not believe what we were hearing.

When I moved to Dearborn, Michigan, I was bullied a lot. The children would pick on me because my mother was American Muslim. I could not believe the ignorance that still surrounded me. Why do people have to be so cruel? In Coldwater, we were being stereotyped because we were Muslims, and when I moved to Dearborn, I was teased because my mom was white. The bullying lasted all the way from middle school until I hit the eleventh grade. That is when I met a couple of good friends that I surrounded myself with. My advice to people is: do not judge a book by its cover and do not judge someone because of their ethnic backgrounds or their religious beliefs. Just because there is one bad apple on a tree does not mean that the apples are all rotten. The majority of the American Muslim population also suffered and was saddened by the loss of lives on that September day.

Being bullied made me who I am today, a better person. I love the diversity in a bigger city verses a small town. I could never be that small-town boy again.

MY FATHER'S SIDE OF THE FAMILY

The first time I went on vacation to Yemen was with my uncle who is my father's brother. My parents did not accompany us, so it was just the three of my younger siblings and me. I was excited to go and finally meet my father's side of the family: my grandparents, aunts, uncles, and cousins. I remember the day my parents drove us to the Detroit Metro Airport. I started to get nervous and excited at the same time because I was going to a different country. I had never been out of the USA before. It was going to be an experience that I would never forget.

As we were saying our goodbyes and started to walk toward the entry gate, I looked back and I could see that my parents were saddened to see us go on vacation without them. They had tears running down their faces. My parents were saddened and excited at the same time for their children to be able to experience such a vacation that kids rarely get to go on.

172

As we sat down at our numbered gate waiting to board the plane for the first time, I spotted an airplane up close. I could not believe how huge it was. When we boarded the airplane, the flight attendants were at the door to greet us, and they were very friendly. It was a long flight. We flew Royal Jordanian, and it was approximately thirteen hours. When we arrived in Jordan, we stayed overnight in a very nice hotel and headed to Yemen the next morning.

When we arrived in Yemen, I smelled diesel lingering in the air. All I heard around me were people speaking Arabic. At that time I only understood very little Arabic. As we landed in Sana'a, Yemen, I noticed there was a different way of getting to the airport. Instead of entering the airport as we would in America, straight from the airplane to the airport, we had to exit the airplane by long tiring stairs to a bus that took us to the airport. While my uncle was gathering our baggage some men came up and asked if he needed some help. When we walked out of the airport, I was very surprised to see my family waiting for us. I could not believe how many family members came to the airport to pick us up. They started to hug and kiss us, and I could not tell who was who.

On our way from the airport to the house, the streets were crowded with people. I could not believe how they drove in Yemen: four people on a motorcycle, kids riding in the trunks of vehicles, horns honking from every direction, no stop signs, and no traffic lights. But, there were police in some areas who directed the traffic. It took around thirty minutes to arrive at the house. There, we were greeted by the rest if the family. I finally got to meet my grandparents. I only heard stories about them before meeting them. My father's family was very welcoming and loving. I had many aunts and uncles and I could not keep track of them.

The homes in Yemen were very different from the homes in America. They were built from rocks and bricks and were beautifully designed. My family wanted to make our vacation memorable. They took us to a different place every day. If it wasn't the park, we would go to the zoo or fair. Furthermore, if it wasn't any of those things, we were going back and forth to the village. The main purpose of taking us to the village was to show us where our father was born and where he grew up. I found the village more beautiful than the capital Sana'a. Farms and huge mountains surrounded the village, which made beautiful scenery. When we were in the village, we got the chance to go mountain climbing. When you go to the top of the mountain and look down, the view of the whole village is breathtaking.

The second vacation in Yemen was in June of 2006, and this time the whole family went. This time it was much better because I was accompanied by my parents and the rest of my siblings. In my second visit to Yemen, I was twelve years of age, and my father allowed me to learn how to drive a stick shift. It was difficult at first, but after I got the hang of the clutch it became easier. I started learning in my grandfather's old truck. The truck was red and looked like a pick-up truck, but a much older version. While we were there on our vacation, we made a visit to the old king's house. It was an enormous house. The king's house was five stories tall and was on the edge of a mountain. The first level had a jail cell where the king would lock people up, but the cell looked cloistered and not very big. Yemen is a very beautiful country, and it holds a lot of history. One would have to see it to believe it.

In 2009, I went for a vacation to Yemen for the third time. On this vacation, we did the same type of things we did on the first visit. However, this time I had the chance to witness a Yemeni wedding firsthand because one of my cousins was getting married. This trip taught me the differences between American weddings and Yemeni weddings. In American weddings, the whole family and their guests gather in one location, and men and woman are mixed. In a Muslim Yemeni wedding, people rent two halls: one hall for the men and one hall for the woman. They do this because the bride cannot be seen by the men who are not from her father's family. The bride's grandfather, father, brothers, uncles from her father's side, and her husband are the only men who could see her. All the woman get together in one hall to party and to congratulate the bride. The same kind of festivities takes place in the men's location. At the end of the night, only the husband comes in the women's hall to take his bride.

My fourth trip to Yemen was in 2013. This was the most memorable trip of all. It was not a normal vacation like before because it resulted in me getting married. At first, I met my wife through family members. We started out by talking on Skype while in the presence of my parents. I was living in America, while she was living in Qatar. We talked for two years and decided that we were interested in each other. We set a date to meet in Yemen to get married because we both had family that lived in Yemen. I decided to graduate first. After I graduated, my family and I traveled to Yemen. Her family came a month later. First, we became engaged. During the time of engagement, we sat with each other and got to know each other better. After a month or so, we had our wedding.

THE INVISIBLE DISEASE

My mother had my baby brother in March 2010. When my brother was a month old, my mother caught bronchitis. She had an infection for about six weeks. She would go back and forth to the doctors getting antibiotics and a cortisone shot. During this time, she had developed a problem with asthma as well. Finally, the bronchitis went away. Although the asthma was still there, my mom started noticing a tingling sensation in both of her hands. She thought it was strange, so she mentioned it to my father. She did not think much of it after, until the next day when the tingling sensation went to both of her feet.

Over a period of five days, more symptoms started evolving. She started to get electric shock sensations from head to toe. She also got muscle spasms all over her body, twitching in her face and heat sensations in her legs. In addition, she had difficulty with swallowing, heart palpitations, and chest pain. After these symptoms appeared suddenly, she knew it was time to go see her doctor. She was so weak she could barely life her arms. After she explained her symptoms to the doctor, the doctor tried to blame it on her hypothyroidism. My mom was confused and felt lost and lonely. At home, I noticed my mother crying every day from the intense pain. She did not want to go to the ER because she feared what the diagnosis would be.

My mother's legs would go numb out of nowhere, while standing. She was so weak, but yet so strong. My father finally convinced my mother to go to the ER. When she went, they gave her a referral to see a neurologist. They ran some blood work for autoimmune disease and did an MRI. When the test results came back and after a few visits to the neurologist, he diagnosed my mom with fibromyalgia. "What a slap in the face that was," my mother told me. Can you believe they never gave my mom a spinal tap? My mother was convinced that she did not have fibromyalgia and went on to see a few more neurologists for second and third opinions.

176

My mother was depressed and struggled daily. She would always be crying because the pain was unbelievable, so excruciating. My father, my siblings, and I tried to comfort her as much as possible. Her family doctor tried to convince her to see a psychologist, and she was very offended. My mother went from being healthy, never complaining about anything, and rarely seeing the doctor to becoming ill. I couldn't believe the doctor thought it was all in her head. After that visit with the doctor, my mom came home saying, "Why in the world would someone want to fake being sick!" She just did not know why the doctor said what they said.

I witnessed the sleepless nights, the daily crying, the muscle spasms, and her falling on the floor because she was too weak to even walk. We all knew that this was not in my mother's head and we would stand by her. After a few years of searching for a neurologist she could trust, she finally found one who gave her hope. She explained all of her symptoms to him, and he could not believe that none of the other doctors ordered a spinal tap. The doctor said that a spinal tap at this stage would be of no use because my mother had been having these symptoms for over a year. After ruling everything out and getting lots of lab work and MRIs done, the neurologist was sure that she contracted Guillain-Barre syndrome. Guillain-Barre syndrome is a rare neurological disorder that occurs sometimes after a viral infection. The body's immune system mistakenly attacks parts of the nervous system. Her neurologist said she was very lucky to be alive. When people contract GBS, they do a spinal tap right away when the symptoms appear, so they can start the treatment. Sadly, my mom did not get one and did not get the treatment. Treatment had to start right away. Without treatment, symptoms could last up to five years or more.

My mother still struggles with symptoms. So far, it has been four years of hell for her. She improved, but the symptoms are still there. I hate to see my mother suffer, and it is very hard seeing her cry all the time and knowing that there is nothing I can do to ease her pain. She still sees the neurologist and is on medication for her symptoms. She is always smiling when she is not crying. She is very hopeful that she will be healthy again. My mother hides her pain behind her smile because she does not want to burden others. During this time, my mother found out who her real friends were. I can tell my mother aged a lot from being sick. I know it takes a toll on someone's body when a person falls ill, but no matter what happens to her, she is beautiful to me and I am proud to call this wonderful woman my mother.

A Plain White Canvas

Mussid Aldubaily

LIFE IN DEARBORN, MICHIGAN

They call me Moose, short for Mussid. I have the privilege of being named after my mother's father. Dearborn, Michigan is my hometown. It is where I was born and raised. I was born the fifth of six children. I came into this world in 1995. I was a ten pound, twenty-one inch chubby, rosy-cheeked baby and I wasn't a difficult one.

"Mother, how was I as a baby?" I ask with a smile on my face.

"You were the sweetest and most active child I've ever had, although you did cry a whole lot and kept me up most of the nights," she said as her tone went from soft to angry.

"Come on mother. Was I that bad?" I said trying to get her to say something positive about me.

"But, then again, as soon as you cracked a smile I forgot all the sleepless nights and back-breaking hours it took me to get go to sleep," she retorted.

"For that I do appreciate everything you've done for me," I said with sincere heartfelt gratitude.

I have always been held to a different standard and expectations were high. After having three girls and a boy, my parents were ecstatic that their hope for another boy was fulfilled when I was born. Being the middle boy has its advantages and disadvantages. Many times I went unnoticed, which worked to my advantage. However, there were times when I took the blame for things that weren't my fault.

Being the baby of the family for eight years, I had the advantage of having the spotlight for a long time. For those glorious eight years, getting my way was easy. You can say I was a bit of a spoiled kid and I was the most loved of the five children. Fortunately, my brothers and sisters loved me just as much as my parents did. In fact, my siblings were also guilty of spoiling me. When reflecting on the eight years that I reigned as the prince of the household, several memories come to mind.

I remember a trip to the carnival with my dad when I was six years old. My dad let me have whatever my heart desired! I went home with a big Grave Digger monster truck remote control car. Although my siblings loved me very much, it is fair to say that when I came home with that monster truck they were all jealous. It didn't help that I gloated about how I was the special one. The spotlight was awesome, and I took advantage of all the toys and trips I took with my dad.

My reign as the prince ended with the birth of my little brother, Abdulghani. He very quickly became the apple of my parents' eye. My little brother Abdulghani managed to suck away all the love and affection that was all mine. My time in the spotlight ended when his life began. Sure I liked becoming a big brother, but that didn't help with the feelings of being yesterday's news. My new reality was that of a middle child. It made me understand how my sister felt being the middle of the girls. The middle child is there but invisible.

It wasn't until the family went to Fairlane Mall as a group that I realized how truly invisible I really was. My aunts and my mom planned on doing a little shopping and letting the kids play in the play area. Great idea—everyone wins! Well, as the hours ticked by, the adults became restless and tired.

They gathered all the kids, or so they thought. The family piled up into three vehicles and went home. They were exhausted! I, on the other hand, was still in the log right smack in the middle of the play area. When I finally crawled out of the log, I looked around for my mom, my aunts, and my cousins. As I scanned the faces around me, I didn't recognize anyone. Panic and fear took over. The little boy who had spent most of his life quiet let out a shriek! Thankfully a friendly security guard took me in her arms and reassured me that someone would come back and get me.

"Your parents love you, and they will be here soon. Don't cry. You're safe and secure with me. See? I've got this badge, and it means I'm mall security and your parents know to come to me to find you," she kept confirming.

"Did you call them?" I asked her with tears in my eyes.

"Yes, sweetie, I did," she lied with a bright smile on her face.

When she realized her words weren't helping, she used a guaranteed strategy to try comforting me. She gave me a balloon, a toy, and candy. Apparently my family didn't even notice that I was missing until they all made it home safe and sound. Everyone got out of the cars, and at some point one of the adults felt it was time to count heads. My father was standing on the front porch waiting for all his kids. He asked my aunts where I was. All three of my aunts started asking one another about my whereabouts.

"I was standing on the porch and as soon as I understood what was going on, I panicked. My boy wasn't there! I jumped in the truck and had no time to wait for anyone. Your grandma came chasing after me, but I left her behind. I was scared of losing you, and your grandma was afraid of what losing you would do to me. She feared I would have a heart attack while driving to the mall," my dad told me later as he was remembering what had happened.

Sure enough, they finally made it to the mall and rushed to the security station. As soon as we made eye contact, tears were running down my cheeks. I was happy to see them. I hugged my dad so hard and I didn't want to let go. Lessons were learned by the whole family that day. We never took a big family trip again without the buddy system in place. My middle sister was my buddy. Looking back, I give my family the benefit of the doubt and I believe them when they tell me it was an accident. Realistically, the two people who would have missed me being there would have been my dad and my sister; neither of whom was there.

After the mall adventure, I had difficulty being left alone. I even cried when my dad dropped me off at school. I thought I was going to be left behind. Thankfully, the fear lessened, and I began to love school again. It helped that my first cousin was in my class. Soon after my recovery, my family moved to Yemen. I was not able to finish second grade because we left before the school year ended.

In July of the year 2000, we went to Yemen for my older sister's wedding. I don't remember much about my first trip but I do remember people making such a big deal over us. I learned the easiest thing for me to do was to quietly follow my dad and brother. Yemen turned out to be fun and interesting. I got the opportunity to experience traditional weddings. I saw the Yemeni tradition of slaughtering cows and sheep in backyards. I saw the different crops the people grew. Yemen is a beautiful place to visit, but I always missed America, the American food, and the American television. We stayed there until the new school year began and we all came back together.

When I was in elementary school, I was like most kids. I had a passion for playing video games, watching as many cartoons as possible, and I thought that girls definitely had cooties. Eventually, Mario Kart evolved into massacre games and Spongebob Squarepants evolved into scary horror movies and cooties no longer existed. I don't remember ever getting sick or being hospitalized except once, when I was nine. I played a game called bulldog with my siblings and cousins. It was like dodgeball, but instead of dodging balls we dodged human beings. We all gathered in the middle of the field and at each end of the field there were two goalies. To get to the safe zone we all had to run to one end of the field dodging the bulldog or goalies. Of course I was the youngest and the slowest and the easiest to catch. Sometimes they took it easy on me and sometimes, by luck, I got away into the safe zone. One day, while playing, the field was muddy and I was trying to dodge the bulldog. I slipped and injured my knee. I cried, but when I got hugs and kisses I forgot the pain. A couple of days later the scrape turned into a blister. Every time someone wanted to examine it I screamed and did not let them touch it. A week later, it got worse, and I developed a fever. My mom took me to the pediatrician, and automatically they rushed me to the Children's Hospital. The doctors diagnosed me with an infection in the knee. I remember the doctors telling my mom, "Had you waited longer, the leg would have gotten infected and may have had to be amputated."

"What is the plan now, Doctor? What can we do to make his knee better and get him home as soon as we can?" my mom asked, looking worried.

"We plan to give him antibiotics and an IV until we see some progress, and with a couple of more exams he may be discharged soon," the doctor answered.

183

"Thank you, Doctor. I really appreciate it," she let out with a sigh of relief.

"You're very welcome," he replied as he was exiting the room.

I was hospitalized for ten days with an IV on me. The nurse cleaned my wound every day until the infection was taken care of. When I was discharged, I was surprised with a welcome home party from my close relatives. It was nice seeing everyone after being in the hospital for so long. I was grateful that it wasn't worse and that I was able to go back to school.

Elementary school years were pretty good. Those days were fun and filled with joy and excitement. I was a carefree kid. No worries in the world. The world revolved around me and nothing else mattered. My friends from elementary years at Salina were the same crew I hang out with today. We have a tight bond. The community we live in all together is a very tight and friendly community. Everyone here cares for the each other; we are like a huge family.

GOING TO A DIFFERENT WORLD

I stayed in school for another three years, and school ended abruptly in 2004 when I finished fifth grade. That was when my family decided to travel back to Yemen. The trip was supposed to be for a couple of months, half a year tops. Instead, my parents decided to take an "early retirement." We stayed in Yemen for SIX YEARS! I left nine years old and came back at the age of fifteen. That was a whole lot of time in a country I had only visited once before. A country that was still strange to me. I met family members who knew me but I barely knew them. I could not understand their language well.

Adjusting to the Yemeni tradition was not hard at all. Basically living in Dearborn made the transition easy because many people, including my family, held on to their religious beliefs and traditions with tight fists. Still there was a huge difference between the United States and Yemen. Yemen had a slightly different dress code. The women cover themselves fully from head to toe and cover their faces with veils. Men wear dress-like uniforms and a jambiya around their waist. A jambiya is a curved dagger, with an animal's horn as the handle attached to a very decorative handmade belt worn for many reasons. Men wear the most expensive, fancy, and elegant jambiyas as an accessory to their clothing on special occasions such as weddings or holidays. The simpler jambiyas are worn on everyday basis in Yemen.

The six years I spent in Yemen were an experience I wouldn't trade for the world. I am very grateful that I was able to go and visit my aunts and uncles, distant cousins, their children, and their grandchildren. A huge clan waited for me there. We lived in both the capital Sana'a and in the village. I liked Sana'a because I got to go to school and learn how to read and write the Arabic language. It was very challenging in the beginning, but I learned to adjust to life there. My main challenge there was adjusting to the time difference. I always had trouble sleeping at night in the first couple of months after we got there. I was like a bat, sleeping during the day and staying up at night. Another challenge was taking baths. In the village, the houses didn't have showers. My aunt would warm up the water on the gas in the kitchen and then bring it to the bathroom for me. I then would mix the hot water with some cold water from the jug in a big plastic container and scoop the water on to myself as I lathered the soap. If I wasn't quick enough the water would get cold and I'd basically walk out shivering.

In Yemen, they had cafes with computers and internet. They also traveled in cars, buses, and taxis. In the village it was a bit different. There, I experienced a completely different world. A hunter's world, I would call it. I pretty much chose the village over Sana'a anytime my parents gave me a choice. We spent most holidays in the village at my grandfather's house where my mom's brother lived with his family.

In the village, I learned how to hunt rabbits, birds, and even laughing hyenas. Hunting was scary at first, but eventually it felt natural to be able to aim at targets and shoot. The most memorable time was when we caught a hyena. Hyenas are very strong, hungry, vicious animals. They are smart animals and that made them worth the challenge.

One day my father, uncle, brother in law, and I got into my father's car. Each of us carried a rifle and a flashlight. We headed towards the mountains at 10:00 p.m. knowing what awaited us in the silent darkness. Each of us planned how the night would play out. Each had an idea. Little did we know that whatever we planned didn't matter much. The night would play out unexpectedly. The adventure was filled with hearts racing and a whole lot of adrenalin rushing. When we finally got to our destination, we set ourselves up side by side with a separation of about two feet in between us. We laid flat on our stomachs and sat down the flashlight by our right arm. The rifles were extended in front of us on the floor. I remember looking through the scope of the rifle into the darkness. I then turned the flashlight on and saw some rocks and shrubs. We laid there in silence only whispering when we had to, just waiting for the hyena to come out of hiding. The flashlight wasn't always on. My dad had a night vision scope that detected when the hyena was around. Once the hyena was detected and it was within the right range, we all aimed the flashlights at it and that caused it to be blinded for a few seconds. These seconds gave us enough time to fire. Once we fired we waited to see if we got him or not. His movement allowed us to determine if he had been hit and injured or if he was dead. Luckily the hyena died on my first time hunting.

After hunting a hyena, we didn't just leave it there. We took it home and skinned it. I didn't do the skinning because it looked so nasty. The hyena smelled so bad. My brother in law did the dirty work. He used a razor and a knife to do precise and careful skinning. He was careful not to cut the fur and ruin it. After the skin is off the skeleton, we would stuff the skin with hay and dirt and then sew it all back up. We then either put it in the tree to dry or on the roof, and it would be a trophy for people to see for months.

Hunting was a fun hobby. On holidays or special occasions we would slaughter lambs and cows. I first slaughtered a lamb at the age of eleven. It was hard and gruesome. My father would encourage me to slaughter lambs along with the village men.

"Be a man and just do it. This is a skill that you will carry on with you for the rest of your life, and you won't have any regrets doing this," he would say.

"But what if I'm not quick enough? What if I don't cut too deep? What if I don't do it right?" I would mumble with a quivering, low voice.

"Stop all your fears and the nonsense questions and just do as the butcher tells you and you will be fine," he abruptly cut me off.

So I did and it was another thing I became very good at. Another thing I got to do in Yemen is drive at the age of thirteen. It is funny looking back at those days now because there is no way my dad would let my little brother behind the wheel at such a young age. Not in America at least.

I had a lot of problems over in Yemen. The main problem was hatred. It turns out that some people in Yemen are not too fond of Yemenis born in America. They have a bad habit of being jealous. People would call me names and make fun of me. The teasing would become an everyday routine. I am a big guy, and compared to the kids in Yemen I look like a giant. So the kids would take it to liberty and point out my weight. One of those days I walked to the market place and I had my cousin with me whom also was blessed with a heavy body as I. We both are also really tall compared to the kids in Yemen, adding to the giant-like effect. As we walked in the dry, hot, exhausting heat, kids would gather and walk behind us, mimicking our moves and walking in a funny way. They threw comments around such as, "Hey, Doob," which meant fatty. I ignored them as much as I could, but when I ignore them, they didn't go away. I waited until they were close enough and made a quick turn on my heel as I swung my arms and grabbed whichever one my hand landed on. No mercy was all I could think of. They pushed the wrong buttons, and I was out for revenge. As puny and weak as they were, they took a good beating. Eventually, the bullying stopped, and I made many friends. It was nice even though most of them became my friends out of fear of me. There was this one person named Murad. I first met him in Yemen. He became my best friend. We did a lot of things together. He showed me around the city. I don't remember all the details about my stay in Yemen but all I know is that I had a lot of fun.

BACK IN DEARBORN, MICHIGAN

Eventually we came back to the United States in 2010. My sisters were all mothers. I was now an uncle. I grew a couple of feet taller and looked totally different from when I left. My family was amazed at how much I changed. I had a hard time adjusting to life in the USA. I got so adapted to life in Yemen; life in America was erased from my memory. I kept the language but forgot how to read and write. A few months after I came back to the United States I was enrolled in high school. I was in my freshmen year. I was enrolled in bilingual classes. My first year was at Edsel Ford High School. Students teased me for being in bilingual classes because I did not know English. They called me a "boater." The word boater is derogatory name directed towards new immigrants who didn't speak the English language correctly. I didn't know how harsh that word was until one day it was directed at me. I was coming out of a bilingual class with a friend I made in that class. One of my childhood friends, I was once close with him, saw me and nudged his friend. They both looked at me and laughed. As they passed me, I heard him whisper, with a very faint light voice, the word "boater." The word felt as if someone took a sharp dagger and stabbed me with it in my heart. I learned from experience that words can hurt more than we expect. I'm pleased to say I've erased the word "boater" from my vocabulary.

I was eventually taken out of bilingual classes. I began mainstream classes in my sophomore year. I also got my first car and first phone that same year. My brother passed down his silver 2000 Lincoln LS to me. That car was once passed down to him from my uncle years before. The Lincoln LS took me back and forth to school and to places to hang out with friends. My dad paid for gas since I had no job and I was still in school. The same arrangement applied to my first phone. My dad gave me his Motorola Droid X and paid the phone bill as well. Basically, up until my sophomore year I had no responsibility. I was given everything I needed. I was a pretty quiet student and I kept to myself. Everything in high school went well except for my grades of course. I didn't pay much attention to class work. I didn't take school seriously. I was very careless and immature. My grades were so bad that by my junior year I dropped out of school. There was no reason to go if I wasn't going to be serious about my future, I thought. I wish someone forced me to stay and finish school, but I don't know if I would have listened to anyone at the time.

Dropping out of school was a bittersweet experience. I got to stay home but I was labeled a drop out. I had to figure my life out. I soon realized that I needed to grow up and find a job. I found my first job at a car wash on Michigan Ave washing cars. It was nice during the summer but brutal during the winter. The pay was low. I was being robbed of my tips by my co-workers. My father had to drop me off and pick me up every day since my car broke down and I wasn't able to fix it. Eventually, I had to sell my car and get something out of it before it became worthless. After a year and a half of working at the carwash, I finally concluded that this job was not for me and I wouldn't want to be stuck in a dead-end job with nowhere to go but backwards.

Eventually my sisters and my parents got to me and showed me how important it was to have an education. I agreed with them. Dropping out and then working at a carwash was the lowest point for me. It made me realize what other potential I may have. That was when I decided I needed to get my GED. Trying to study for the GED was a bit challenging since I hadn't done too well in school. I couldn't do it on my own. So I went to the Arab Community Center for Economic and Social Services (A.C.C.E.S.S.) and asked to be tutored. I stayed in tutoring for a couple of months and then took the GED test after I felt comfortable that I could pass. Like many things

190

before, the test was also a challenge for me. I worked hard for a little over six months until I finally got my GED certificate.

Because I was planning to go to college, I needed a car. To get a car I needed another job. My brother told me about a job opening at Ford Motor Company. I applied and was called in the week after. It is a good solid job for now. I plan to keep the job at Ford until I'm able to succeed and climb the ladder to a higher position. About three months after having my dad drop me off and pick me up at the job, I was able to save up and buy a car. I dipped into my bank account and pulled out what money I saved along with the money my father gave me and I bought yet another Lincoln LS. This time it was a 2006 creamy-colored beauty. My new car was one hot, smooth ride that turned heads when I drove by.

I never got any tickets or got in any trouble driving except for once. The tires that were on the car at the time weren't meant for the winter weather. I was driving with my friends under the bridge on Rotunda road going to Tim Horton's for some coffee. I glanced into my rearview mirror and saw a black Mustang speeding and passing everyone in its way. He tried to cut me off. In my head, I thought there was no way this guy was going to pass me and get away with it. I floored the gas pedal and sped up and caught up with him. He sped up more than me, and so the race began. The race was going well until the infamous Michigan potholes came into play. I tried to maneuver the car, but it was too late. I hit the pothole, and the car slipped. I lost control of the car. It spun in circles and came to an end by smashing into a speed limit sign. When we finally stopped, I looked around and saw my friends were okay with their jaws dropped to the floor and stunned by what had just happed. We were a bit shaky but thankful we were all okay. I had to call my dad and let him know what happened. I got in trouble, and the keys were taken away from me until I was able to fix the door, the fender, and the bumper. That was the first and last time I ever drove recklessly.

While working at Ford I decided to apply for college. I'm majoring in mechanical engineering. Juggling a job and an education is a bit difficult, but it's teaching me to be more responsible and to work hard for what I need. I will always have my family around to help me when I need them, but at the same time I'm growing and will soon have to be the man of the house. Applying to college opened a new door in my life. It is like having someone put a plain white canvas in front of me and letting me paint my future. I'm pretty sure it will get messy before I see beautiful art in front of me. But I know I will work hard for my future and build it up to be the best it can be. I eventually hope to get married and have children and live a happy prosperous life.

Through a Thunderstorm Comes a Rainbow

Amanda Nicoletti

This journey started on November 9, 1990, when a bouncing baby girl by the name of Amanda Kaitlyn Nicoletti was born to Jo and James Nicoletti at 4:01pm at Henry Ford Hospital in Detroit, Michigan. As a child, and through my teens, I grew up in Detroit. My mother worked for an insurance company, and my father worked for a very successful trucking company. From the very outset, life was a struggle for me. I was born with a blood infection, and none of my doctors or nurses thought I would make it through the night. With prayers and my mother's faith, I am today 23 years old. My mother was very determined to make sure with everything in her power that I would make it through. Just four years before me, on June 6th 1986, she had a miscarriage with my older brother Jeremy; she didn't want to risk losing another baby. Coming home from the hospital, I was instantly glued to my grandmothers Judy and Claudette whom I called Mammy and Granny respectively. Growing up, I was rarely at home with my parents. I was always with my grandmothers.

At a very young age, my Mammy had me in church attending Sunday school services and church-related activities such as choir and plays. To continue keeping me in the church, I was placed in a Christian school starting from the first grade all the way up to my sophomore year in high school. For the most part, I had a pretty normal childhood. In the fifth grade, my whole life started to turn back upside down. Mammy had passed away while she was in the hospital for an infection, and Aunt Patty passed because of cancer. It had become very hard on all of the family, and that's when the family began to drift and fall apart. Mammy and Aunt Patty were the glue that held us all together. To this very day, life is not the way it once was.

Shortly after their deaths, my dad was in the hospital going through kidney failure and amputation of his left big toe. He was a diabetic and had adverse reaction to medication. After my dad got home and got better, things began to change. With all of this happening, many family secrets began to come out of the closet. One of these secrets changed my life forever. The one person I would least expect it to happen from my very own father. Things began to grow more distant and awkward as the days went by in my house. My mom and dad were either fighting or not speaking at all. At one point, it had gotten so bad that my mom started sleeping on the couch just to get away from my dad. Everyone around started asking questions such as why my parents were always fighting, but no one knew why. My mother had suspected, and then she discovered that my father was having an affair and with his best friend's sister. She was his ex-girlfriend from before my parents had met. They started seeing each other after her grandmother's funeral.

My dad had gone on a camping trip. That gave my mom time to figure out what she was going to do when my dad came home. At this time, I had no idea what was going on. All I knew was that my mom was very angry. When my dad pulled into the driveway and my mom ran towards the front door, I was sitting on the stairs of my bedroom waiting to see what was going to happen. I was very scared. When my dad walked in the door I heard my mom yelling and asking him, "Why would you do this to your family?" and, "Is she going to take care of you the way I did for the past 20 years?" After she confronted him, he tried to deny. But once he realized that my mom knew everything, it finally hit him. As he walked down the hall to their bedroom, he looked at me and said, "Baby, I'm sorry." He went in the room, threw a suitcase on the bed, packed some of his stuff, and left. This left me wondering, "Is he ever coming back? Why would he do this to us?"

After all of the back and forth, my parents filed for divorce on February 19, 2007. My dad did not really want the divorce, but my mom decided that she was not going to live with a mistake that he had made. She had told him, "Love doesn't live here anymore." After the papers were filed, she had him come and get the rest of his stuff. That very night, my mom called my Granny who was living in Kentucky at the time and asked her to come and live with us. The next day we left and made the eight and a half hour drive to bring Granny to Michigan.

After that, difficult issues began to surface. When my father left me and my mom, financial burdens started weighing heavily on us. We lost the house where I grew up. He did not hand over the papers we needed to keep the house, and we were forced to move out.

My mother, Granny, and I found a house in Dearborn. We moved and we tried to start our new lives. I grew a lot of hatred towards my dad because of lies, such as where he really was, how he claimed he and his girlfriend were just friends, and what he was putting my mom and me through. I could not wrap my head around the fact that he had left us for another woman. In an effort to keep the peace between my parents, I tried to split time between my parents and act like nothing was wrong. The struggle in having to do a week with my mom then a week with my dad became hard and unrealistic. The fights were getting worse, and they both wanted to get information out of me about the other. During one of my weeks with my dad, my mom had come over to drop some of my clothes off. My mom and dad got into a huge fight because my mom found out my dad was taking me over to his new girlfriend's house, the only thing my mother begged him not to do when he left. My dad was standing on the front porch yelling, "She is my daughter too, and I will take her wherever I want."

"So she can brainwash my daughter?" My mother asked angrily. After she had said that, my dad did not reply. He just walked back into the house; my mom gave me a kiss, got into her car and left. My life felt like it was completely turned upside down. At school, my grades and attendance were slipping. Consequently, I dropped out of school in tenth grade.

I was fifteen years old when I had my first job as a waitress in Dearborn and I began to take online courses to obtain my high school diploma. Because my dad stopped paying my tuition, my old school put a hold on my transcripts. That gave me the chance to graduate a year earlier than I was supposed to. I had my high school diploma on September 5, 2008.

At an early age, I had to learn responsibility. I had to learn how to make money and how to take care of a household. Sometimes it took a toll on me but in the end it only made me a better and a stronger person. I learned how my mother must have felt with me growing up because for a while I was in her shoes. I was able to learn how to budget and save money. Because of all this pressure, I became depressed. I lost focus and my condition got so bad that I even began to question my faith and whether there really was a God. I knew that these questions disappointed some people. My father wasn't very happy with the decisions that I made. I stopped the week-to-week visits and solely moved in with my mom. I kind of thought that moving with my mom would be better for me because when I was with him he was rarely at home. He was always with his girlfriend and her three children. I felt neglected and out of place. There came a time where things got mentally and physically abusive, and I could no longer take it, so living with my mom I thought was the best thing I could do for myself.

The battles in court became too much to handle. I began to feel that I didn't belong with my dad. I started feeling that my dad left my mom because of me. My father was a very jealous man especially when it came to me. Because my mother loved me very much, my dad felt that my mom chose me over him. After I moved back home, I had to see doctors about depression. I couldn't pull myself out of depression without the help of someone else. When I was able to get myself together, my mom started slipping into depression. She barely ate or slept. She always seemed to be quiet, kept to herself, or cried. It took her a very long time to get over certain things. She stayed strong for me, but it was her time to break down.

I had trust issues when it came to everyone around me especially in relationships. I was lacking trust and I was always suspicious because of what had happened to me. Through this whole ordeal, I was only able to trust two men in my life. Those me were my uncles, Jeff and Josh. To this day they are the only ones I truly confided in until I started seeing Edward. We were together for over two years. In the beginning, I thought I could open up and get over the trust issues. Everything was great. It went as far as moving in together. I thought that might be my happy ending. Boy was I wrong. I started finding out different things here and there, and all the fears came rushing back at me. The relationship became abusive and loveless. He was constantly lying and cheating. I kept trying to remind myself of how I needed to get myself away from this pattern yet again.

Our relationship got worse. He was constantly in and out of jail because of drugs. He was a big pill user. One night, when I went home from class, I found him drugged up on Xanax and Vicodin. He was very incoherent. We got into an argument over our relationship and his drug use. At the time, he had me believe that he chose our relationship and he promised to flush what was left of the pills down the toilet. As I begged him to stop, he stormed out of the house. Later that night, around 11:00 p.m., the cops were knocking on the front door. Ed had been picked up for walking in the middle of traffic in Lincoln Park. He had the remainder of the pills into the bottom of a Nike bag, which he always carried. He had supposedly flushed out those pills in the toilet. He was taken to Oakwood Hospital and placed under evaluation and then he was released. Around 3:00 a.m., he came storming through the front door and woke me up. The argument continued. I had found the other pills he had been hiding. I tried to run upstairs to flush them by myself, but he grabbed me and dragged me down the basement stairs. He was hitting my head on the way down. I had to fight him off and run to call the cops. When the cops arrived he was taken into custody and placed in the back of a cop car. I will never forget the last look he gave me through the back window of the police car as they drove away.

The next day I had to go to the police station and place a written statement to get a restraining order. After that night, I never wanted to see him again. A few short days later, I received a notice to appear in court because I was pressing charges. He had to serve 18 months for domestic violence. After our relationship ended, I was depressed to the point of overdosing. I thought I was the reason for him being the way he was. After realizing that I had more to live for than being a waitress, I decided to do more with my life. That was when I enrolled in Baker College of Allen Park to study Surgical Technology. During my second semester of college, things began to fall apart again. While I was in class, I received a phone call saying that Granny was being rushed to the hospital because she had a massive heart attack, had to have an emergency surgery, and had to have two stents placed into her heart to open the arteries. I felt like I was about to lose my best friend, but it seems that difficulties make me stronger. That same year I had the opportunity to get my finances straight. I was working two jobs, one at Target and the other at Subway. My mom, Granny, and I moved to Detroit and bought a house over on the Eastside that was more affordable. I finally began to feel that things were looking better.

New struggles began just shortly after moving. My mom was working for an insurance company called Amerisure. When that company started downsizing, my mom was laid off. Being laid off cause her to become depressed again and placed a lot of pressure on me to hold the household together. At this time, I was still working two jobs and attending college full time. This began to take a toll on me. I was constantly tired, worn out, and emotional but I never let it show. I tried my best to find some type of balance, but just sometimes it didn't work out in my favor. I really didn't have a personal life because I was way too busy handling my business and I could not find many people of my age that I could relate to. A few times, it had cost me friendships. I didn't know many eighteen or nineteen year olds who had to hold down a household and try to make a life for themselves. Yes, it was a hard struggle and sometimes I wanted to throw the towel in, but I did not. I learned to push through and handle everything without a single complaint. A few months later things began to look better. My mom got a job working six days a week at an appliance store in Detroit. I was able to kind of relax and not stress as much.

As I was in college, I realized that I wasn't in the field I wanted to get into. I started researching different schools and that was when I came across Sanford Brown College in Dearborn. I always knew in my heart I wanted to work in a hospital setting to help people and save lives. I weighed my options and I left Baker College. I then enrolled into Sanford Brown as a medical assistant on April 4, 2012. I finally felt as if that was what I wanted to do for the rest of my life. Learning how to help people and learning more about the body and its functions just seemed so amazing to me. Having a dream of working in the medical field made me feel as if I had some type of purpose. Through school, I was able to do an externship for experience and I did very well. April 20, 2013, I graduated with honors as a medical assistant and I couldn't be happier.

Shortly after graduation, I had the opportunity through the school to take my state board test. Despite the struggles and stress, on November 15, 2013, I passed my state board test. Not long after that, I had my first job working in a family clinic in Allen Park, MI. As things began to brighten up in my life, certain things began to crumble again. After six years of barely talking to my dad, I found out that he became very sick and he had a stroke that left half of his body nearly paralyzed.

Finding that out hit me like a ton of bricks. I had to sit back and realize that it was time to let go of the past and move forward. I realized it was time for us to try to rebuild our relationship again. After a few conversations my dad had owned up to what he had done to me in the past. He admitted to certain things that I wasn't too sure about and answered a lot of questions that I had. Still feeling very hesitant and scared of my dad, I was willing to open up and be around my father. To this very day, we make sure we talk to one another every day and catch up on events that had gone on throughout our days; we even do Sunday dinners together.

Through letting go and seeing how much my dad changed, I am at a point in my life where I can begin to trust and open up again. I was able to find someone that I could fully open up to and trust. It had taken a lot for me to come out of my shell and fully open up. I am currently in a healthy and loving relationship. For a little over five years, I have been with a wonderful man named Kayamone Sutton. There definitely had been difficulties due to my past, but he has been very understanding and has stood by me through it all. The most magical day of my life happened on March 18, 2013. That was when I was asked to become Mrs. Sutton. I currently reside in Redford, Michigan with my very large family. Sometimes it gets crazy but I wouldn't have it any other way.

Through all these trials in my life, I have learned that the only one I can really count on is me and my will to try to reach for the stars. When things fell apart I was able to use that as motivation and get things going for me. To this day, I push myself to be all that I can be and not let anything hold me back. I am currently attending Henry Ford Community College to obtain my nursing degree. Someday, I hope to be working in a hospital as an RN in the pediatric ward.

Life As I Know It

RAE 'SHAUNA SPEARMON

Cheers and applause surrounded a room at Hutzel Hospital as a beautiful baby girl was born. The Toliver and the Spearmon families gathered together on the day of September 22, 1993, to see this new life. A new life that no one knew would turn out the way it did. Looking back of course, I do not recall much from that day but I have seen plenty of pictures that gave an idea about it.

As a child, I was always with my grandparents on my father's side. They always spoiled me and never said no to anything I wanted. Until I was four, I was the only child and grandchild. My mother decided to get pregnant with my little sister, Miyah. She did not get to meet my grandfather though because he passed away when she was only seven months old. After this tragedy, I started looking at the world differently, or maybe I was just maturing.

After my grandfather passed, I started to cling on to my grandmother more. Everywhere she went, I was right there behind her. As a child, I always thought I was quite popular. This popularity came from having drug-dealing grandparents. My grandma started going into business for herself when she lost her soul mate. Her business didn't stop her from taking me with her wherever she went. I was on her like white on rice until I started school. I fell in love with school from the first day I started it. It was fun, creative, and I always learned something new. When my mom dressed me she reminded me how

203

I was the cutest little person with very high fashion. That was always nice of her, but when it came to school and learning it was my aunt Delilah who always helped me. She attended all my parent-teacher conferences, school activities, and enrolled me in extracurricular activities.

My favorite teacher was my first grade teacher, Mrs. Green. She was like family to me, and my family loved her as well as she loved us. With the assistance of my aunt, Mrs. Green and I exchanged holiday gifts every holiday.

After school, I was enrolled in cheerleading. I cheered for the West Seven Rams on Seven Mile Road in Detroit. My aunt assisted me in learning the cheers and making up new ones. My cheer coaches loved my aunt and me. Often times they tried to get her to fill in for them on days they couldn't make it. I cheered for around three years until I had to stop because my grandma was moving off Seven Mile.

My grandma inherited my great- and great-great grandma's house. They lived there together and when they died, they left the house for my grandma. My aunt and her daughter, Jaszmin, had come to stay with us for a short period. Jaszmin and Miyah were like vinegar and water half the time and two peas in a pod the other half. They're the same age with a three month difference. My grandma and I were hardly there, so she didn't really mind the company. We were always out handling business. That was until I was about seven years old. I was legally taken from my grandma's house to go with my mother.

My younger sister, Miyah, had a god mama named Jamie who used to adopt different kids, but they would not last long. I personally did not care for her growing up. I always thought she was a curmudgeon. One day she called my grandma's house and told her to bring me over there. My granny hung up the phone then she looked at me and said, "Baby, do you want to go over Jamie's house today?"

Of course I said no, and my dad added his two cents.

"Well, she don't have to go if she don't want to."

Therefore, my granny called her back and they had a very short conversation. Jamie was mad though. I got to hear the whole thing because my granny put the phone on speaker.

"Hello, yeah she said she don't want to go, so she's not coming over there today maybe next time," Granny said in a challenging tone of voice.

"What! How? You just gonna let her tell you what she wanna to or not wanna do?" Jamie said angrily.

"First, honey don't yell at me. Rae' Shauna is my grand-baby, not yours, correct? Last, what I do over here is what I do, so she's not coming. Have a good day and goodbye," Granny said.

She hung up the phone. I do not know what went on before that conversation or after it, but what I do know is that next morning I was awakened out of my sleep and carried to the front door. A figure was holding my arms and making me wake up all the way up. After I was fully awake I realized I was being escorted out of the house and off the porch by a police officer.

"Get your hands off me, woman. I don't know you, and right now I don't like you," I shouted as I tried to snatch away from her hold. I started yelling, screaming, and kicking. I even fell to the ground and had a temper tantrum. My grandma tried to come after me but she was stopped by some oversized policeman. I was having so much of a fit that I didn't realize I was being taken to my mom's car. Everything became a blur for a few minutes because all I remember after that was driving in the car with my mom, stepdad, and sister. By the time I snapped back to reality I was at my cousins' house with my sister. My mom and stepdad must have gone somewhere. About an hour had passed when my stepdad came in the house with a deep cut over his eye and was slightly bleeding; not too bad though but as a kid it was more than enough for me. My biological father had found my stepdad when he was on the way to my cousin's house in my mom's little red car. My stepdad said that he and my father had gotten into a fight and my dad's car swiped him and forced the car between the wall under the bridge and my grandma's truck that my dad was driving. Once they both managed to get out of the cars my dad and my stepdad started fighting and my father hit my stepfather with an empty beer bottle that was laying on the side of the road. Looking back on that, I still wonder why neither one of them had a run in with the police right then for fighting in the middle of Plymouth in front of the police station. Somehow, the fight was broken up and ended. My dad went his way, while my step dad continued to my cousins' house, a few blocks down. My family called my mother, and she had gotten there pretty fast. Things kind of went into a blur for me after that.

I found out later that my mom and dad were fighting over my custody. Well it was really my grandma and my aunt Delilah; my dad didn't do much. They lost the case, and my ma was granted full custody of me. Why were they fighting over me but not my little sister also? Well that's because my dad didn't think my sister was his when my mom was pregnant, and he had gotten another lady pregnant at the same time. Although he didn't claim her either until she was around seven or eight, I can say that once my sister Miyah was born he started to claim her. I had a chance to talk to him about that, and he said that was because Miyah looked exactly how I did when I was born but my other sister Kyra looked different. I

206

said to him, "Stupid, she has a different mother. Of course she not gonna look like us."

My mom sometimes told us that we looked like him when we made a stupid face and we were in trouble. Living with my mom was cool and I had an awesome childhood. For a while, it seemed like we moved a lot. We were staying in my deceased grandfathers' house on my dad's side, but they eventually made my mother move and my aunt Delilah took her place. We moved around from house to house after that because my mother did not like the neighborhood, or she simply did not feel like the house was a home.

When I was in the third grade, we moved into a house that my grandfather's wife on my mothers' side had owned. She decided to rent it out to my mom. It was a nice house and it was big. Everyone had their own room. I think mine was the biggest only because I had a queen-sized bed and a twin-sized bed with more room left over. My sister and I became known around the neighborhood because of our bad attitude problems and our loving personalities. Also, everyone went to the same school around the corner. I became best friends with one of the girls in my class. She also stayed around the corner from me and she too had a loving personality with a bad attitude to offset it. Miyah and my friend's younger sister became good friends as well. We were always together and were thick as thieves until she moved away. I was sad for a while because I lost my best friend but I eventually got over it and made new associates. It took a lot for me to call someone my friend. My family was big enough so I did not need too many of those.

Six or seven months after my best friend moved, we moved, too. My grandfather passed away, and his wife started treating his kids differently. I didn't have to deal with her because I was only a child but I did see what she was doing and how conniving she had become. She hurt my feelings when she told me she sold my grandpa's house. He always told my when I was younger that one day his house will be mine and not just the upstairs where my room was. He always followed that by saying, "That's when I'm gone away though baby girl, so let's hope it won't be soon."

I just listened to him talk while he smoked his cigar and had an occasional drink. My grandfather used to work at Ford Motor Company before he retired. He did as much as he could while still teaching his children and grandchildren to be independent. He started my mother off with an apartment when she was pregnant with me. Because she was only seventeen and a few months from her graduation, he wanted to make sure she didn't lose focus. He put her in the building with my aunt, her second oldest sister. The oldest sister moved to Ohio to change her environment. She lived down there until a few years ago when my mom cogently asked her to come back to Detroit. While she was in Ohio we visited her every holiday, summer, and some weekends as well. My mother made sure to keep up with her sisters, brothers, and other family members whether in state or out of state. She was a family woman and loved all of them. They too loved her children; even my stepdad was loved as if he was born into the family.

By the time I was in the sixth grade, my mother stopped renting and bought her own house. We all loved it. She looked at us with a joyful smile and said, "Now this is home." When my mother bought the house it was livable but not completely renovated. That didn't stop us from moving in it. We fixed the other minor details and remodeled it while staying there. Just before I switched to the school down the street, I had gotten into a fight with some older girls who jumped me. The school was trying to kick me out. My mother was very angry because the school wanted to kick me out and let the other girls stay. She stopped what she was doing and came to school. When she got there, I was thinking to myself, "This lady is crazy!"

She came in the school with a screwdriver, ready for anything. That was not all she had. Her firearm was in the car because she was not allowed to bring it in the school. She also had our dog in the car. Our dog's name was Bones, and she was a full-blown pit that we kept in the dark. The only people she was allowed to see were my mother, stepfather, my sister, and me. My mother was thinking, "My daughter just got jumped by some bigger kids; now let me prepare myself because their mama better not try to say anything when I'm going off on them." My mother and father had extremely bad tempers and the smallest things had them black out on a person, especially if that person was a nonfactor to either one of them.

My mother pulled my sister out of school early and took us home. We spent our winter break in Atlanta with some of our family. Upon returning to Detroit, we enrolled in our new school close to home. For a while, we were the new kids in the school and on the block. At school, everyone tried to feel and see what kind of person the new kid was. My little sister didn't care. She was going off on people as soon as she got into her classes. On the other hand, I let students wonder and whisper amongst themselves. For some reason a girl decided she didn't like me and wanted to fight me. Everyone came and told me this on my first day.

"Tell her I'm not scared. We're in the same class. Don't wait until school gets out because I'm not waiting around. If she wants to fight, I'm not hard to find," I told them to tell her.

After lunch that day, she had people tell me to meet her in the bathroom. "Now who in their right mind is going to walk into that set up?" I thought.

209

As I suspected, she was in there with all her friends. I didn't go in. I only saw them because someone walking next to me went in there. I was standing in the hall waiting on her to come out and approach me. She finally got my message and walked out of the bathroom. Of course, she was trying to be all big and bad but never coming in my comfort zone. After she was done wasting her time and energy doing all that yelling, I simply asked her, "Are you going to fight me or keep talking?" She tried to swing and missed because I moved away from her punch allowing myself to give her the business.

I was not kicked out because it was my first day and I evidently didn't start anything, but they did call my mom on the number she gave them. Eventually my mom became known by all the staff who worked at the school. Whenever my sister or I got in trouble with someone from the staff who did not know my mom, we were sent to the office. The office sent us back to class and told us, "Do not do it again. We don't want your mom up here showing out on you."

My seventh grade year she actually did show out and I was a little embarrassed. I was suspended still from school. I did not tell anyone and no one knew until my little sister was suspended as well. When she got in trouble, they called my mother to get her out of school for the rest of the day, and she could not come back until she was off suspension. Upon my mother's arrival, one of the people who worked in the office told her, "I know you're mad both of your daughters are suspended." BOOM! Just like that, I was busted.

I was in the lunchroom when everyone kept coming up to me saying, "You better run. Your mama up here." My fellow classmates were afraid of my mom when she was mad, but they loved her when she was feeling fine. I thought they were playing because they were all talking about sneaking down the back stairs instead of going with the rest of the students. To my surprise, there she was standing at the door of the lunchroom. My heart sank a little, but it was too late to turn around now, even though I still tried. She yelled out my name and said, "Bring your ass here now." I tried to think of a plan but I was quickly backhanded into the elevator door that was directly across from the lunchroom. I wasn't embarrassed too much because I had too much fear of my mother's wrath. When I came back from my suspension, all the students were approaching me telling me how I was a trooper and how they were scared for me. I just laughed and that was all I could do in response. I loved my mother; she wasn't abusive. She just disciplined her children as needed.

As a family, the four of us always took trips and went on vacations. Every summer we went to different states, amusement parks, or something of that nature. We rarely went to the same place. If we wanted to go back to a certain place, it was at a different time. One summer we sold candy and she sold dinners. Although it was all fun and games for us, she was teaching us values and how to be independent. The next year we went to Michigan Adventures and Kentucky with the money we made. We had a blast when we were there. As the summer was coming to an end, I was getting excited because I was going to be an eighth-grader. I was looking forward to being in the highest grade in the school and enjoying all of the activities they were having.

When my eighth grade year first began, I loved it all except for one class because my teacher was cruel and mean. She didn't like any of her students. As the school year went on I eventually learned how to deal with her. Even though I did not really care for the lady and she was a rough teacher, I didn't let that affect my grades. I was always on top of my work. That made her ease up on me just a little, and I was happy about that. As much as I enjoyed school, I had to take a few days off because my family and I were in a very bad car accident.

On February 14, 2007, we had a snow day at school. It didn't really look bad outside and my mother decided to take us to C.C.'s Pizza, but that came to an end when we were on our way there and a truck hit us from behind. We were at the light and sitting in our suburban truck. As soon as my stepdad lifted his foot off the brake, a big impact came upon us. I heard my sister scream just before I felt the impact, but that's because she said she saw it coming before it happened. She was always being extra nosey about something and just so happened to be looking out the review window behind us. When the vehicle hit us, the back window shattered and the back of the car lifted up. As soon as the car dropped back down I tried to jump out of it, unaware that we were still rolling from the impact. When I opened my door my mother yelled, "Wait Rae' Shauna! Don't hop out of this car yet." If it wasn't for the fact that my arm was stuck in between the seats, I probably wouldn't have heard her.

After the car came to a stop we didn't have to call the police because he was sitting at the light on patrol when it happened. He made a call to the EMS and the fire department. My younger sister was rushed to the hospital because she was having severe abdominal pain. My mom went with her while my stepdad and I stayed back and waited for my aunt to get there to take us to the hospital. The policeman tried to figure out how it happened and file his report. My mother was furious because her children were hurt. She tried to fight the man but the policeman wouldn't let her. When asked about the accident, the guy who hit us said he looked down for a hot second and the next thing he knew he was in our rear end. My aunt took my stepdad and me to the hospital. My mom, step dad, and I were seen and released that day, but we were worried about my little sister. The hospital admitted her because she had a bruised liver and blood in her urine. They wanted to make sure nothing else was wrong. The hospital had released her the next day. We stayed up half the night talking on the phone with her because she was scared to go to sleep while no one was there.

In the morning, I was awakened early by my parents to pick my sister up from the hospital and hear what they had to say. My mother's friend Jamie took us to the hospital in Garden City. We were hurting very bad. My mom, stepdad, and I didn't feel the pain at the time of the accident because our adrenalin was rushing. When we arrived at Garden City Hospital we all took many x-rays and scans. My mother filed a lawsuit against the guy. I had to get surgery on my wrist because of some torn ligaments and ripped tissue from the accident. My mother and I had to do constant MRIs. When my little sister told the doctor she had stopped hurting, my mother told her she should not have done that. Not only because she wouldn't get anything from the lawyers, but because she would feel the pain a little later in life. That was true because now she does complain about having some severe pains that your average sixteen-year-old should not have. After the lawsuit was settled my mother set it up so that I would get my money when I turned eighteen. If she didn't do it that way the lawyers would put my portion of the lawsuit money in with theirs as one lump sum. My mother didn't agree with that, so she made special arrangements for me. The lawsuit took a very long time. I was in the ninth grade when we finally settled.

I was nervous about going to high school. I told my aunt how scared I was, and she told me not to go off someone else's judgment. She told me I had to make my own. I used to watch different shows on TV. That made me think high school was just like the way it was on TV. I was the oldest sibling and my cousins were older or younger, and generations change. Therefore I didn't know exactly how it was going to go. In my mind I was going to this big school with a cast on my arm, not knowing anyone, and I was at the bottom of the chart again.

My first day was better than I expected, thanks to my mother. I went in the school and instantly became cool with many people. All the seniors thought I was a very short senior that wore wicked hair styles. My mother told me as long as I maintained a 2.5 GPA or better I could get my hair done every week. My hair dresser was her longtime friend Jamie Woods. Jamie and my mom would do hair shows together; her hands were blessed with a gift.

In my ninth grade year I was a subtle young lady. I did not do much and tried keeping to myself, but for some reason everyone wanted to be a friend of mine. I didn't get involved in extracurricular activities in high school until my sophomore year when I developed school spirit as well. I was enthusiastic about my school. I played every sport while I was there except basketball. I just could not get jiggy with that. I loved to watch the games while I cheered on the side, and half time was the best. I also ran track, danced, played volleyball, and softball, which was my favorite sport. Every time I joined a team there was a stereotype, especially when I joined the cheer and dance team. Since a lot of people knew what I was capable of, there wasn't much stereotyping during my junior year of school. During my entire life, I never was the typical slim girl that everyone expected or looked for in society. As a child on the cheer team for the West Seven Rams, I was a chubby little girl. Because of my weight, everyone thought that I could not keep up or I was not fit for anything. Every time I proved them wrong. I've heard people whisper when our school was at an away event, "They have a big girl on their team. She probably can't jump high or flip around with the dances or cheers, but then again she's not really fat she just has some chubbiness to her."

"You're right, but we will see when the game or show starts."

To their surprise, I was better than the average skinny girls were on either team. In addition to that, I loved being on different teams because of the support I always received from my mother. She and my stepfather were at every game. My little sister would come along as well unless she was too tired to stay awake or did not want to sit out in the sun on a hot day. All but a few loved my mother; every team called her "team mom," even my instructors and coaches loved her. The only people that did not really like her were the ones who could not take the constructive criticism. They thought she was to mean and blunt. Of course she always spoke her mind and never held back a thought. My best friend, Felisha, loved her as if she was another mother to her. Felisha and I had met in ninth grade year through our mutual friend Daniesha, who had moved away again in our junior year.

Felisha and I were thick as thieves. In school, you did not see one without seeing the other. All of our classes were at the same time, which was good for me because she made school fun. For example, everything was a competition. She made a game out of everything. Some of our fellow classmates got mad and called us teacher's pets because we had the highest grades in the class, and if there was an extra credit assignment, we did it because we were in competition. She became more than just my school friend. We were friends outside of school as well. We always hung heavy and had a lot of fun. It was not just us, though. She had sisters who also had a few friends along with our other mutual friends. We got together to go hang out somewhere and sometimes we just stayed home and relaxed but still had fun. Her dad was famous for throwing card parties, and we put together a game night for our friends who didn't play cards. After she met her mom, my mom had no problem with me going over her house or her coming over mine.

In my junior year, my life turned around and took a nosedive. My mother died right before my eyes. We played a softball game at Central High School, and the bad part about it was that we had lost the game. After the game, when everyone was leaving there was a strong wind that came along with a weird feeling. It blew like a tornado and made our stomachs clench. After the game my mom, step dad, aunt, and I decided to go over my cousins' house and have a little fun. We picked my sister up from home because she stayed after school to catch up on some work with a teacher. My mom rode around looking for her, but she took another route home and the very last time my mother circled the neighborhood she said, "If I don't see her she's going to be left home until we get back later."

Right after my mom said that, we saw her walking down the street from over the log cabin bridge.

When we arrived at my cousins' house I decided to go outside and play around with my younger cousins. All the adults left to make a run to the party store. Upon their arrival back to the house, everyone was getting their items and putting the others out on the table. As she was taking out her items, my mother said, "whoa" as if she had gotten dizzy, then passed out on the floor. In a state of shock, the Payday I had just eaten came back up in vomit. My stepdad was trying to do CPR but was not doing it right. I took over, and my mother had a strong pulse. The house was frantic. My cousin ran to the back screaming and could not bear to watch. My older cousin came from her room upstairs holding a check on her pulse. My younger cousins were screaming and crying while my aunt, younger sister, and stepdad were hysterical. When the ambulance came they took over, and she peed her pants. They took her to the hospital. On the ride there, I asked if she was okay. The paramedics told me she was breathing on her own, but when we arrived at the hospital, I was told she was dead on arrival.

After everyone was called to the hospital, no one believed that this horrific situation happened; they arrived at the hospital swiftly. It was especially hard because Mother's Day was a couple of days later and we had something big planned for her. After we left the hospital, we told our family we wanted everything to stay the same. As soon as that was said, everyone agreed but no one seemed to listen. They didn't allow me or my sister to leave with my stepdad that night. We were told he was in an unstable mind, so some of the guys in my family took him out somewhere while we were being pulled around. Everyone wanted us to come over to his or her house. For the first couple of days my sister and I jumped from house to house because everyone wanted us with them. After a while, we went to our cousin's house that my mom was extremely close with and looked up to. My stepdad, sister, and I all stayed with her for a little over two weeks. We couldn't bare going home; it just didn't feel right.

We went to the house to grab a few clothes or things that we needed. The trip was in and out within five minutes tops. After the memorial service, we went home and tried to put our life back together as best as we could, but that did not last long because my mother's oldest sister came and took us away from my stepdad. She made me and Miyah move with her. Of course everyone knew that if something was to ever to happen to my mother that's who we were to go with, but we wanted to stay where we were. Once we moved with our aunt, that left my stepfather with no one but the dogs, alone in what we called home. Every time we saw him in the mornings before school, the loneliness still showed within him. My senior year came around and I had to switch schools because my school closed after my junior year.

This was the hardest for me because my mother and I always talked about how things were going to be during my senior year and how extravagant prom was going to be. I still had a nice time; it was very fun and its memory will stay with me forever. On the day of my graduation I just couldn't stop crying. During the ceremony, the choir sang a song my mom would say was sung at her graduation. Some of my fellow classmates thought I was crying because we were graduating, but those who really knew me personally knew why I was really crying. I had developed a cold heart for people after losing my backbone (mom). It was like I didn't know how to love anymore. After a while I had gotten into a relationship and somehow I allowed him into my heart. When I realized I had fallen in love, it became very hard for me. I started asking myself, "How did this happen? How did I allow someone in?" Because in my mind I forgot how to love, I often found myself pushing him away. As much as I pushed him away, he seemed to keep holding on to me. He found me every time I tried to be alone to cry or release that anger I had inside of me.

In a way, my boyfriend seemed to help me with dealing with my grief. Although he did not know it, the support, love, and dedication he showed me was what kept me going strong in the face of all the obstacles that I had. He gave me the strength and courage that I looked for if my mom was still alive. I really needed this support to deal with all the pressure I have, along with keeping a keen eye on my younger sister and trying to accomplish my own goals in life and graduate from college.

A Wolf in Sheep Clothing

Ali Nasser

RELIEF

I finally had him in my arms. Staring straight in his eyes, my anger fully maxed out as I punched him repeatedly, thinking of my next move. Should I go through with what I came to do? I start to wonder if I should bring myself down to this level of inhumanity, or if I should go on letting this man live knowing I let him live. If I let this man live for another day, will my self-less regret continue every day? I know he has a son at school right now. If I kill this man, I might just create another me. If I kill this man, I might just end his son's life of happiness. My eyes were sanguine red as if they were Lucifer's eyes. I felt like a fallen angel set out for vengeance. All was silent except for a distinct ring in my ear canal. Bam! I pulled the trigger. Don't judge me yet. Read on and you will understand.

BEGINNINGS

My mother was a very hard-working person who had to deal with having me when she was sixteen. She was forced to drop out of school to provide for my well-being by working full time. Also, my dad worked full time at a Chrysler plant. He still works there today. As a baby, I really do not remember much but from what I saw. My parents loved me and did anything to provide for me.

I was always remembered as a quiet child in elementary school. In my preschool, Detroit Academy, I always minded my own business and played with my own blocks. I didn't bother others and I didn't take other children's toys. I was just calm and well behaved. When my classmates took my toys, I just sat there and watched. I was not sad or angry; I just didn't mind letting them play with my toys.

I can remember myself sitting for hours playing Super Mario on my green Gameboy. I don't think I really cared about school, but my mother always pushed me to know my ABC's and take care of my work before thinking of having fun. Doing my homework and handling my business first was what I did under my mother's supervision. Doing this everyday soon became a habit. Every day my mom picked me up from my first grade class and took me home. This routine was followed daily until middle school.

THE TABLES TURN

As a seventh grader, I spent most of the day with my grandmother Maria. We loved going Downtown (Detroit). We used to take a bus and it seemed like no matter what we did, we found a way to have fun even when we were lost in Downtown. My grandma and I went to carnivals and bought the greatest roasted peanuts. We were always happy. One day, we missed the bus and things weren't going so good for us because it was dark out there. While waiting for the bus, I really had to go pee. There were no bathrooms near. I walked down to the street corner between two buildings and I started relieving myself.

That was when I started to hear shouting. I looked down the street towards the bus stop and I noticed a car full of people yelling with two men in front of the fruit market on John R. I would never forget the image of the black Chevy Malibu that was on the street at that time.

"You f—in in the wrong hood my nigga," a man in the black Chevy shouted.

"You got me f—ed up," one man shouted right back at him from the street corner.

A man in a red hoodie started to walk toward the car slowly from the opposite side of the fruit market. He pulled out his mac 11 and started spraying (shooting) toward the car. At the same time, the two men in the car whipped out their pistols and started spraying from the car. Shot after shot, bullet caps flying everywhere, every man in the car was dead. After witnessing such action, I was sent in shock. I looked for my grandmother and started running toward her with a speed I never thought I could reach. On reaching the scene, I found my grandmother on the ground with two bullet holes in her chest. I stood over her and cried silently. As the puddle of blood grew bigger and bigger, so did my anger for the three gangbangers who killed her. I stood next to the bus stop as I watched them pull the bloody bodies out of the black Chevy.

HIGH SCHOOL

High school was it all. It was money, cars, girls, and drugs. Coming in as a normal high school student and as young as fifteen, I still was a quiet kid with just a bad past. I really didn't care for school. I just knew that I had to finish high school and any school beyond that wasn't going to happen for me even if

223

my parents told me to do so. As a freshman, I didn't know a lot of people, and this was the time when I got involved with the wrong crowd.

First day at school I just happened to be the first in class because I didn't have anybody to meet or see. I was sitting there. Everyone came in with a friend. They took up the tables around me. The late kids came in and took the last two seats next to me. Their names were Jake and Josh. Judging by their late arrival, I guessed that these kids didn't care for school, just like me. Soon, I got to know the two, and believe me, we really got to know each other because we had been through it all. We three became the richest kids in the school. Everyone knew us because we were where the drugs were.

Fights were becoming normal throughout the year, but never inside the school. People didn't always make payments, and when they didn't an ass kicking was coming their way.

"Big Joe owes us money and he always with his boys out of school, so we need to get him now or never. He won't expect it," Josh says and we agree.

Tick tock the clock was ticking. Jake, Josh and I were waiting for big Joe to get out of class because he owed us more than 50 bucks. That was a new Gucci (high end company) belt to me. Ding-dong; class was out.

"There's Joe," Jake shouted.

Joe turned to see who shouted his name and bam! Josh knocked the "socks off" of Big Joe. As I watched, Josh yelled, "Let's go empty this nigga's pockets." I did; then we just walked out of school. I felt like I accomplished something great at the time. We got way more then what Joe owed us.

The next day came, and consequences were running through my mind, "Are they gonna call us down?" It was just my luck. "Ali, to the office," the teacher shouted. I feared the dreadful walk down to the principal's office. What are my parents going to say when they find out? I had never been in trouble at school. Will I have to deal with all my unfortunate decisions now? As I walked down to the principal's office, I contemplated whether I should continue my journey to the office or if I should take my chances and run. The decision was tough, but in the end I decided I should carry on and face the outcomes of my choices like a man. Moreover, after everything I had been through, I was the man. Who could touch me? As I turned the corner in the hallway, I ran into Jake and Josh. I quickly felt a rush of relief burst through me. We quickly began to brainstorm a story that we all could agree on before entering the office. After all, he was not the nicest principal out there. We decided to dodge all the accusations and deny any violence on our part. We quickly walked into the office and saw the anger and fury written all over the Assistant Principal's face. He asked us to have a seat and then one by one he asked us to tell the story from our viewpoint. As Jake and Josh began to tell their stories, I prayed that our stories would match up. Thankfully, the principal believed our tale and told us to return to our class and stay out of trouble. The sense of relief that came across me was evident. I just felt a rush of excitement and I almost didn't even feel bad about the lie that we told. Walking out of the office, we felt like free men walking out of prison. It was a win-win situation for us. We escaped the consequences and we had an iPhone in our pockets along with the $200 that we stole from him.

As the days passed on, I grew closer and closer with Jake and Josh. We began to see crazy amounts of money. I was part of their business but never did I smoke the weed myself. I thought about how great the money was for me. I made a lot of money and I made it fast. This was a dream come true for any teenager. I couldn't resist. I could make money without all the hard work, and on top of that, I would not deal with tax money being taken. My favorite part about this job was that I never had to deal with a boss. We were our own bosses. We did not need to answer to anyone.

As time went by, we were beginning to buy expensive things. I decided to buy myself a $4,000 Movado watch. I still have it until today. We decided to fly under the radar. We had to stop buying expensive things and lower the attention on us. My new goal was to buy a car. By the time tenth grade rolled around, I wanted to be the first in my class to have a nice car. With all this money, I felt that I had to show off.

When tenth grade came around, I was rolling in my brand new Cadillac DTS. With a car like this, I felt invincible. All the kids wanted a ride in it, and I got extra attention from girls. Although I had a lot of girls all over me, I was not interested in any because I had already fallen in love. I had met a beautiful girl, and we were great together. Here's the story about how I met her. One night, Jake and Josh picked me up and took me to a club. They had already prepared our fake IDs and we were ready to have a blast. We walked into the club, the music was just right, and the people were all hyped up. As we began to party, I noticed a cute girl from across the club. For a minute, we just stared at each other, and then I made it my goal to give her my number. As I made my way through the club, I noticed that she kept her eye on me. I finally went up to her and we danced for a little bit before we finally talked and exchanged phone numbers. Her name was Nancy, but she went by the name Nana. We started to hang out a lot, and I began to like her. Eventually, we dated and we kept a relationship going for a long time. She was with me through everything except the undercover business I had.

One day, my friends and I were kicking it back and enjoying our lives. We ordered pizza because we were extremely hungry. The pizza arrived, and we sent Josh to grab it. We smashed all the food that we got and then we just chilled. Josh went into the kitchen to wash his hands. When he came back, he pulled out a gun and waved it around. He tried to show me his new "toy" that he bought. I froze for a moment because I realized that I was not on board with the idea of guns. We argued about it for a while but we came to the decision that weapons were necessary. We needed to have protection at all times. I still needed time to think about this and so I walked out and I decided to stay away from my associates for a while. I took a few weeks to myself. After a few weeks of thinking about it, I decided that I loved the fast money and maybe they were right. We did need to be protected at all times. Later on in the week, I ran into the guys at school and we fell right back into the same patterns as before. We were partying and enjoying the perks of our job.

It was close to the end of the school year, and we were at the top of our game. We decided to expand our business. This was risky because we were putting ourselves in a tough situation. We had to become more aware of our deals. Our name was spread all around the city. When people wanted good "stuff," they came to us. Everything was going great for me except for my family life. I grew distant from my family, and my mom was constantly suspicious. I chose this life for myself and I could not turn back. Now that we decided to expand, I came up with the idea of having people work for us. Jake and Josh did not like this idea until I talked them into it. I convinced them that we could pay someone to do the dealing for us and we make most of the money. They did not like the idea of bringing anyone else into the business, but we decided to go through and expand.

We recruited a freshman kid named Mike. We chose Mike because he was young and naïve. We paid him a little bit to get the job done, and he was not capable of betraying us. He was excited to begin working, and we sent him on his first mission to test his loyalty. Mike had to deal drugs to a customer that always tried not to pay. This was a test for Mike. If Mike was able to deliver the drugs and receive the payment from him, then we were in business. Mike went on his mission and completed it successfully. With Mike on our team, it was easier for us to fly under the radar. We did not have to do the dealing anymore. Time went on, and we were doing great. We were at the end of our year and we had become huge in our city. This was when I began to question whether all the money and the recognition was worth it.

I began to think about my grandmother and the guys who shot her. Every time I carried that gun, I was playing the same role my grandma's killers played. I began to feel like a monster. How could I have witnessed such a tragedy and yet I continue on this path. I was in love with the fast life. It became my addiction. I could feel the rush I had when I pulled the stacks out of my pocket. The person I had become over the years was not me, I thought. Suddenly I was struck with a thought. The guy that shot my grandmother is still out there somewhere, roaming freely. This thought made me angry. I wondered if I would ever get justice for my grandmother. Will I ever see this man again? I wanted to run into him one day. I can almost taste how sweet his ass kicking would feel. I became more and more eager to find him someday. If he sees the person I had become, he would be intimidated, very intimidated.

Thursday morning, I woke up a little bit later than I usually did. I saw twenty missed calls and twenty-seven text messages from the guys. It had to be urgent. I opened the texts and began reading them. The first few were text messages saying that they were outside and they were trying to pick me up. They said they needed to pick up their money from someone who had robbed them. One of the texts told me to be prepared. I quickly called them back. No answer. I tried calling them time after time. Every time I called, I was directed to their voicemail. My mind began to wonder on. I was worried that they ran into some kind of trouble. What if they got shot or killed? I shook those terrible thoughts off and I threw on some clothes, grabbed my car keys, and rushed through the door. The first place I decided to look for them was their home. As I was pulling up in front of their house, I noticed that their car was not in the driveway. This was automatically a red flag to me. The house also looked different. It looked empty. Their parents were probably out too. I was feeling a little confused. I did not know where to look or who to ask. After driving around for a few hours, I decided to go back home and wait for any answers. No call back and no texts from them. They were nowhere to be found. I went to bed and I tried to think positive.

The next morning I jumped out of bed because I heard a loud knock on my front door.

"Open up. It's the police."

The police! I was panicking. Immediately I started to hide all my money and all the items that might look suspicious. Again, I heard the knock on the door and I rushed down. Thankfully, my parents were both at work and I was home alone. I rushed down and I opened the door.

"Ali Nasser?" asked the tall, buff cop.

"Uh, yes, I am him," I replied nervously.

My thoughts were racing. This was it. I was going to jail for a long time. What would my parents think? What would the kids at school say? Nancy came to my mind right away. What would she think or do when she finds out?

The cop put a picture in my face. Because of my nervousness, I did not recognize the faces. I took a second look and I could almost hear my heart dropping into the pit of my stomach.

"Do you know these boys?" said the female cop.

I hesitated whether I should say yes or no. I do know them. The boys in the picture were Jake and Josh. Why are the cops asking me about them? Maybe they went missing. Or maybe they caught them with the drugs. My thoughts roamed as I replied to the cops, "Yes."

"And how do you know them? Are you close friends with them?' asked the male cop.

"I go to school with them. Nothing really close; just my classmates," I said trying to look calm.

I played it smart. The cops thanked me and told me if I saw them anytime soon to notify the police right away. When I asked why, they said they could not say but they were missing. They were on the run. I was desperate for answers. As soon as the cops drove away, a thought struck me. I ran into my car and I drove to Mike's house. His parents answered the door and told me that Mike was out with some friends at a hookah lounge. I thanked them and left. I drove around and called Mike repeatedly. He was not answering me. I made a round back through the hookah lounges we usually sit at and I spot Mike's car. I go in and I notice him sitting with a group of people. As soon as he makes eye contact with me he begins heading for the back exit. I walk toward him, and he looks back and then begins running toward the door. I am confused. Why is Mike running from me? What does he know or should I say what did he do?

I spotted a few guys I knew from school, and they were looking at me in a weird way. I asked one of them if they had seen or heard anything from Jake and Josh.

"Haven't you heard?" He asked me in a surprised look.

"Heard what?" I asked.

"Word on the street is that Jake and Josh were into some illegal shit and someone snitched them out," he murmured.

"Who snitched?" I asked angrily.

"Word is your boy Mike snitched them out," he murmured again as he looked around checking the surroundings.

I said to myself, "Mike? I am shocked! Mike would never have snitched. This couldn't be true. If Mike snitched, why didn't he tell on me?" Now I needed to find Mike. As I was walking to my car, my cell phone started ringing. I did not recognize the number but I answered anyway. It was Josh. He asked me to meet him at the local park. I met up with him later on that day and we ended up talking about everything. He told me that they were snitched out about the weapons they had because they were not registered. They did not want to go to jail for ten years so they decided to run away. He asked me to help them out. "I will see what I can do," I said before I left.

Soon after that, I found comfort in my girlfriend. My girlfriend and I were hanging out a lot, and I began to forget about Jake and Josh. I just didn't want to be part of that life anymore. I was not interested in that kind of life anymore. That was not me anymore.

One day, I left my phone lying around, and Nancy and I were hanging out. I went down to the store and I left my phone. When I came back into the car Nancy was upset. She asked me to take her home, and I was just confused. I was shocked and I asked her why. She said she knew what I was into and what I had been doing and she did not want to be with a drug dealer. I swore to her that I had not been doing that in a long time and that it was the past, but she did not believe me. She stormed out on me. I could not believe that she left me. I tried hard to contact her but she never answered and that was the last I heard from her.

After Nancy left me, I could do nothing but regret my past. My past caught up with me, and I never thought it would because I had been out of that lifestyle for a while. I decided to change for the better and it was not enough. I had nothing left. After all the years of selling the drugs but never using them, I felt I should turn to them now. Maybe I should try weed. I heard it made users feel good and it was a stress reliever. Maybe, just maybe, it was not such a bad idea. I thought about it for a few weeks. I did have a little bit hidden in my bedroom. I always saved it in case I needed some extra cash fast. I did not want to hear from Jake and Josh again because they would only bring me down more. God knows who helped those boys out. I knew that I needed to focus on myself and that was exactly what I did. The next morning, I woke up and I was feeling somewhat hopeless. Without even thinking, I walked over to my dresser, uncovered the little stash, and put it in my pocket. I told my parents that I was going to the library to finish some homework. I rushed out and I made a stop at the gas station. I bought a rello. I was going to smoke weed for the first time. I ran into my car and I parked in a place where no one could see me. That was the moment when I went against all my moral values. I rolled up the weed and I lit it up. I took my first puff. I choked on the first time but then I got the hang of it. I felt like I was on cloud nine. It was as if I didn't have any problem in the world. For some reason, when I was smoking, I began to think of my grandma again. This triggered my imagination. I was zoned out and I felt like everything was a dream. . . .

I finally had him in my arms. Staring straight in his eyes, my anger fully maxed out as I punched him repeatedly, thinking of my next move. Should I go through with what I came to do? I start to wonder if I should bring myself down to this level of inhumanity, or if I should go on letting this man live knowing I let him live. If I let this man live for another day, will my selfless regret continue every day? I know he has a son at school right now. If I kill this man, I might just create another me. If I kill this man, I might just end his son's life of happiness. My eyes were sanguine red as if they were Lucifer's eyes.

After this experience of imagining having my grandmother's shooter in my hands, I realized it was not worth it at all. I made the decision to forgive him. People make bad decisions just as I did. I felt like I shouldn't hold a grudge. I decided that this path was not the path that I wanted for my future. I threw out the drugs and I got rid of the gun. I decided that I needed to make myself somebody and to continue my education. I graduated high school and here I am at Henry Ford College writing this story. I chose the title *A Wolf in Sheep Clothing* because nobody knows the path I walked and the obstacles that I had to overcome. I hope you do not misjudge me like what other people did.

She

Rasha Chehab

~~~~~

FANTASY LAND

She walks down the riverside to see the flowers blossoming and the sun beaming. As she looks up, the sky begins to move and the ground begins to shake. The clouds burst, and everything around her begins to disappear.

"WAKE UP WAKE UP!" She gets up only to see blackness. She goes downstairs, kisses her mother goodbye, and walks to school. Dark minds fill the classroom. There is nothing but silence. She walks home from school.

"STOP," her mother yells, "YOU. YOU CAUSED ALL THIS."

BAM! The door shuts. Silence everywhere. Walking into the room, she looks at a figure with beastly beauty.

"Good and evil live together?" she wonders. Everywhere she goes, she hears two little angels murmuring in her ears.

"STOP! IT'S NOT RIGHT TO THINK THIS WAY," says one.

"DO NOT LISTEN, HONEY. DO IT ANYWAY," says the other.

She brushes one shoulder off.

"Angel, keep me with you. I choose you."

"But, my dear, I am no angel. Haven't you heard of the devil in disguise? Oh, we'll be the best of friends."

She walks with the devil everywhere she goes.

"No sun in sight. The world is a cold place, my angel, but with you I'll be all right."

She walks home again. She rushes to her room. A soothing gust of wind fills the room.

"Ah! Silence, my dear. How do you feel? Do you hear the silence? Do you feel . . .?"

"NO!" she cries.

"Go, my dear, go. I will see you soon. Now close your eyes," says the devil. She opens her eyes to find herself sitting on a bridge right above the river with her feet dangling. She smells the ordinary smell of flowers.

"Think! Think! How did I get here? I see no darkness!"

How magical it is to find a happy place! She closes her eyes in her happy place. There is still no darkness. She jumps in the river. Wherever the river takes her, that's where she wants to go. The river stops flowing. Suddenly the water clears and she sees herself standing on stones. These are no ordinary stones. They are colorful and shiny. She picks one up. A beam of light shoots up.

"What's under there?" She picks up more stones only to see a completely new world.

"What? These are kids running and I'm not alone! This better be real!" she says. After removing enough stones, she jumps into the hole and into the new world. She starts singing and laughing. She is making a new friend. Her name is Angel.

"This is my happy place. I don't ever want to leave," she says.

"WAKE UP. WAKE UP!"

She opens her eyes. Bam! She's 18 and all grown up. Sunlight is shining through the crack in the dark room. She leaves her room.

BETWEEN TWO WORLDS

Life around her went from black to grey. Is this a little color change? Could I be feeling happy? Silence filled the house; she was all alone. She got dressed and took a nice long walk. I walked down the same street; I see her. I see her, but only this time she was smiling. She and I became closer than ever. We then learned to live together. She would get up every morning and look in the mirror, only to find me.

Day by day, things get worse and day by day, but she gets better. Every day she goes for a walk, still trying to figure herself out. Every day her world wears a different color. Today, she is out for a walk. The sun is out, and she realizes it looks like the world of her fantasy, except this time it is real. Rainbow stones and all those colorful flowers fill her eyes with light. She wakes up and smiles.

She closes her eyes and sees herself talking to many young people. Ten years pass by. "It's a lonely and very cold world. You feel things you shouldn't have to feel, but you will only grow and learn to be happy if you look at the bright side of things and stay positive. Learn from all your mistakes. It's never too late for change. You create your own happiness, and I found mine. Today I live for what really matters and I am happy because I choose to be happy," she says.

She hears claps, gets her belongings, and a little girl runs up and grabs her leg. "Come on, Mommy, Dad is waiting outside."

A few weeks later her daughter asks, "Mommy, why did you name me Angel?"

"Well, when I was about your age, every time I closed my eyes I saw an angel. That angel and I became the best of friends. I hated waking up because then the angel would be gone. When I had you, every time I opened my eyes my little angel was right beside me."

She woke up from her dream realizing that she was I and I had only been dreaming for a long time. I woke up realizing I never looked at the realistic side of things. As a little girl, I had a big imagination. I always thought too much, and it distracted me from many things. Because of my insecurities, I guarded myself from many things. Everything was always bottled inside because I never knew how to open up to people, not even to myself. I put up a wall, and I denied that I would deny everything. I believed that no one wanted to be nice to me when I was the only one who wasn't nice to me.

I remember it as if it was yesterday. Waking up every morning, my mom and I would get into such a pointless argument. I admit that back then my mother wasn't at the top of my list and I felt as if she hated me because she was nicer to my other sisters than she was to me. Sometimes I would let out things like "Why can't you be like Dad?" My dad and I were close, and she hated it. That was probably the reason why she fought with him and me all the time. I am realizing now that she didn't mean to do what she did, because she was stressed out.

One day, I walked inside my house and went to the basement. I saw my mom hitting my older sister who was in the fifth grade. I didn't know what to do. I just sat on the steps and watched her, but I hid so she wouldn't see me. Back when we were younger, my mother wasn't an abuser, but she laid her hands on us quite often. No one had gotten it worse than my older sister had. Maybe Mom hit us because she was new at being a mother or because she was unhappy with my dad. She let it all out on my older sister. One time, my dad came home while she was hitting my sister, and he went off on mom.

When we were younger, we didn't know Dad well. He was not around as much as he should have been because work was his priority, and when he got off, he went out for a smoke or to play cards with his friends. He had three jobs. We rarely saw him, and that was probably what caused all the fights between him and my mom. As soon as he got home, all we heard was yelling and things being thrown, but we never really did anything.

When my dad was younger and able to smoke, it was the same routine every day. When he decided to come home, he and my mother would argue for hours. He would throw everything around because, no matter how mad he was at her, he never laid a finger on her. After they finished their argument, he would take me along with him for a drive, and he smoked one cigarette after another. He opened up to me about his feelings. Later on, my parents fought because my mother thought that I liked my dad more than her. She thought that because I always described him as my best friend. I did love my mom. I never told her that enough. I'm sure she knew it, but she was never sure of it. I just wasn't as close with her as I was with my dad.

One time, my grandparents, my dad's brother, and dad's uncle were over. I was inside with my sisters, brother, and cousins when we heard screaming outside. My mom ran inside after a short while. She was throwing everything around, and my father followed her inside. I guess they fought because, she said, my dad didn't defend her when my uncle made a smart comment to her in front of everyone. After that, my parents kept going at it. Eventually it led them to wanting a divorce. When they had the papers, we tried keeping my little sister from knowing. When she eventually found out, she cried hard, and we were sad about it, but all they did was fight. We didn't talk to our parents for a good month. They always made comments like, "If it wasn't for you guys, we wouldn't be together." Or, when Mom said, "I wish I never had you." We would get mad at such comments, but we never took it to heart because we knew everything came out of anger. They didn't end up getting a divorce, but my mom didn't talk to my dad for the longest time.

Years passed, and things were the way they were up until I was in the tenth grade. My mother was pregnant, and she kept it away from everyone for about two months because she was embarrassed. She cried every day. My youngest sister gave her a hard time about it saying, "Mom, you're so embarrassing." The rest of us were excited, and we told our youngest sister to shut her mouth so that my mother wouldn't feel worse about it. Five months into her pregnancy, she grew to love the baby. We were all excited, and we found out she was having a boy. My dad was the happiest out of all of us because he always wanted another son, and she never agreed to have more children. Nine months and a week or two went by. It was a Thursday night, July 22, 2010. My mother felt pain in her stomach. My dad wanted to take her to the hospital, but she said it was fine, and she brushed him off. That night, we put the baby's bed next to mom's bed because she felt she was ready to go into labor at any time. They next morning, my older sister woke me up and said, "Mom is going into labor. Even though her water didn't break, she wanted to have the baby." I was excited and I called my brother. He was at the barbershop with my neighbor. When I told him the news, he was happy. We called our relatives because we were excited. I got up and cleaned the house. My aunt came over to help out.

A couple of hours later, while I was tidying up the house, my dad texted me saying that the baby had passed. I went into shock and started crying. My sister started yelling at me because she thought I misunderstood what he was saying. I called my dad, and he confirmed the news. Even though my dad thought that I was the only one who could handle such news, I took it the hardest. Crying my eyes out, I called my brother and my sister's best friend, Lena. Lena rushed over and drove me to the hospital because my older sister couldn't be around a sad environment. In the hospital room, everyone was sad except my mom. She was holding the baby and playing with him as if he was alive. We knew she was traumatized so we didn't say anything. Everyone in the room was heartbroken at the sight of my mom. We named the baby Hussein after my grandfather who had passed. When I took the baby and held him, I started bawling my eyes out. I felt as if he was alive. He looked peaceful and beautiful. When my brother took him away from me, my mom started laughing and asked me why I was crying. When she said nothing was wrong with the baby, I cried even harder. I knew that she had gone into shock. I left the room for a while. As I went back in, the doctor came in and asked to take the baby. My mom said she needed a few more minutes. Everyone walked out of the room except my brother, Lena, and I. All of a sudden my mom started crying hard, and she held the baby close to her and wouldn't let go. The doctor came in and took the baby. My mother became depressed and couldn't walk. My brother held her and drove her home that night. Lena and I went home before mom, and we saw my aunt cleaning out all of the baby's supplies so that my mom would not see them and become sadder. When my mom arrived, she went crazy and told my aunt to put everything back.

The next day, my mom made a doll and dressed it up in my brother's clothes. She used his picture for the doll's face and put his baby hat on top. It looked like a real baby. Everyone tried to talk to her and tell her that it wasn't right, but it was as if she couldn't even hear us talking to her. She was traumatized. This went on for about two months before she let go. She kept all his things in a cabinet which we weren't allowed to touch. Months passed by before our family grew closer.

Two years later, everyone went back to what we normally did. I'm in college now, and I work as much as I can. My brother works day and night, and so does my older sister. Their main priority is money. They don't bother going to school. My youngest sister is now in the tenth grade. Because money is tight with my dad, we all work for our own money. Things are very hard because recently both of my dad's parents died from cancer. Our closest uncle has cancer. The dad of my closest friend, Alisar, died two days ago from cancer, and it was devastating. Today we do what needs to be done, but we are thankful for what we have. We live and learn day by day hoping to advance ourselves. I hope that one day I succeed in what I need to do in order to repay my parents for everything they have ever done for us. Life will go on, and I'm terrified of what the future may hold.

Stare

BILL TURBETT

~~~~~~~~

"Hi there. Uh, well, no; I'm not quite ready to order. Maybe you could bring me a coffee, black, regular while I look at the menu? Great. Thanks."

I wonder why that woman over there in the corner booth is looking at me. I don't think I know her. Do I know her? No way; I'm sure I've never laid eyes on her before. Just ignore her and check out the menu.

I wish she wouldn't keep staring at me like that.

"Ah, yes, I'd like the Reuben sandwich with French fries, please, and would you make that the beef Reuben, not the turkey, please? Great. Thanks."

She's still staring at me. What the heck is going on? I'm sure I don't know her. She doesn't seem to know me. At least I don't sense any recognition in her glance; she is simply staring at me. Very disconcerting. What is it that she's seeing, or thinks she is seeing? My god, I wish she would stop looking.

Maybe she thinks she knows me.

I don't know her, that's for sure. I'll just look away. Maybe she'll quit staring at me. But I suspect she thinks she knows me.

It's funny how you sometimes run into people you think you know, or more likely, who think they know you. Like that time at the Dearborn Performing Arts, when that lovely African-American lady greeted me so warmly. She certainly thought she knew me, that's for sure, but I had never seen her before; I'm quite sure of that. Still, she was such a knockout, I sure wish I had known her. She was on some guy's arm, though. So I just gave her a bright smile and a nod, held eye-contact for precisely one and a quarter seconds, and passed on. Well, what else could I have done? Had I let it go any further I'd have had to admit I didn't know her from Adam. Then we would both have been embarrassed.

I'll just casually let my glance wander around the dining room and slip past the corner booth. Yep, she's still looking over this way. Oh, thank god; here's my waitress.

"Ah, there we are. Mmm, that looks good. No, that's fine; I'm all set, I think. Well, you could top up my coffee, next time you have the pot in your hand."

Well, at least I've got something else to focus my attention on instead of that woman in the corner booth. I'll call her 'She Who Must Be Ignored'.

Looks like the waitress has brought her a meal, and she's shifted her attention to the food, so I can study her for a few seconds without her staring back at me. Aged sixty to sixty-five or so; trim figure, not overweight; hair blondish, turning grey. Medium height, I'd say, dressed conservatively but not unstylishly. Do I know anyone who fits that profile? Nope. At least, I don't think so.

I realize I'm getting on, so by definition I'm becoming forgetful. But I'm not losing it, at least I don't think I am, and I definitely don't know that lady. A certain amount of forgetfulness is normal, sure. I'm always running into people who think they know me, but once we've compared notes, it always turns out they don't. I think I must have one of those faces. Call it a generic face, nothing outstanding about it, just a very ordinary face, a face in the crowd, as they say. But quite often, I meet people who think we've met before.

244

Maybe it's a matter of eye contact. Some races are big into eye contact and some aren't. In the Tony Hillerman novels, the author, who writes about life on the Navajo Indian reservation in Arizona and New Mexico, describes the Navajo as being very uncomfortable with direct eye contact. He says they don't like it at all and it is considered impolite to look too directly at a Navajo, although the one time I actually met a Navajo he didn't seem at all uncomfortable. Just looked ordinary. That was when we were driving the motorhome to California and one of the rear tires blew out just the other side of Holbrook, Arizona. But, come to think of it, the guy who came out to fix the blow-out was an Apache, not Navajo. Still, it is probably a similar culture. Arabs, on the other hand, are into serious eye contact; sometimes it makes me a little uncomfortable. I know I tend to hold eye contact for a bit longer than some people are comfortable with, but when I'm speaking about something important with Arabs, they seem to be looking directly into my soul.

This dolly isn't Navajo, though, that's for sure. When I look back at her, she doesn't look away; just keeps staring. And I don't think she's an Arab; if she is, she's completely Americanized, I would say. She isn't wearing hijab but Western dress, with some make-up, and a little décolleté showing. Yeah, she's European-American for certain. Is she starting to look familiar, or have I just been looking at her too much? There seems to be something about the way she is holding her fork with the little finger curled outward that rings a bell.

I don't see any wedding ring, but that doesn't mean anything in this day and age. This is the era of women's liberation, after all. Lots of women don't wear a wedding band today. Neither do men, for that matter. She seems confident

245

and self-possessed, though she sits with her back to the corner, which could be a defensive posture. She hasn't cracked a smile since I first noticed her, so I would conclude she is a serious-minded person. Next time we make full eye contact I'll give her a little smile. I'll hit her with my tentative, little-boy smile, which always works with "women of a certain age," as the French say. There. Hmm, no response whatever. Now that is interesting.

Perhaps she is just lonely. Yes, that's it; she is eating alone, so maybe it's just that she's lonely. Since I have to eat alone so often, I know what it is like to feel uncomfortable eating by yourself in public. You feel so conspicuous, as if everybody is looking at you. I'll keep my gaze focused over her way and watch for an opportunity to smile, so she won't feel so uncomfortable.

Uh-oh. Somebody's joining her. Looks like it could be her daughter. Well, at least she's talking. Suddenly the conversation is becoming very animated. Must be a relief after sitting there in silence for so long. But she keeps looking back at me. I'm getting embarrassed with this. Is it just me?

All right, here comes the waitress with her check. She's giving the waitress some bills. At last! Relief is in sight.

What's this? The daughter, or whatever, is helping her up. . . . Oh my god! OH MY GOD! The woman is grabbing a white cane from the seat beside her. She's blind! Oh, what a total ass I am. The poor creature is totally blind.